The Caravan Gang
Holiday Park Rescue

Anthony Lugo

Illustrated by Steve Mills

This edition published 2017 by mardibooks
www.mardibooks.com

ISBN 978-1-909227-79-8

Copyright © Anthony Lugo 2017

Illustrations © Steve Mills 2015

The rights of Anthony Lugo to be identified as the author of this work have been asserted by him in accordance with the Copyright, Designs and Patents Act 1988.

All rights reserved. No part of this publication may be reproduced, stored in or introduced into a retrieval system, or transmitted, in any form, or by any means (electronic, mechanical, photocopying, recording or otherwise) without the prior written permission of the publisher. Any person who does any unauthorised act in relation to this publication may be liable to criminal prosecution and civil claims for damages.

All characters and places in this book are fictitious, and any resemblance to any persons, living or dead, is purely coincidental.

A CIP catalogue record for this book is available from the British Library.

Dedication

I would like to thank a few people who supported me with writing this book:

For giving me the talent and the knowledge from an early age, my father Douglas.

For allowing me the time and money to proceed with my daft idea and the patients to put up with me in general, my wife Caron.

For bringing my characters to life a great artist, Steve Mills.

To anyone who takes the time to read this book and hopefully likes it, thank you so much.

Anthony Lugo
September 2017

mardibooks has a small but growing stable of writers from around the world.
We publish in ebook format on Amazon and hard copy
To find out more visit: www.mardibooks.co.uk
This book is also available from Amazon as an ebook.

About the Author

I am 48 years old and a qualified mental health nurse currently managing a team looking after people with mental health problems. I have wanted to write a book for over 15 years. I love the adventure and the surprise when I have written something that comes from out of the blue. I love to be funny and adventurous. Humour, I think, is my strong point and finding good characters. My experience in mental health has definitely helped there. I also run a small bed and breakfast in the country with my wife, Caron, who puts up with my humour and allows me my writing time. We have been married for 10 years and have 6 children between us – more inspiration for characters.

My father used to buy me comics every week. Famous Five stories were a great influence.

Anthony Lugo
October 2015

Preface

Venture off the beaten track to a park hidden away from ordinary folk; a park sheltering a number of peculiar, rather talkative friends, which just so happen to be caravans.

Named "Holly Bush" and a sanctuary for travellers of all ages, the park is home to a family of friends, owned by Mr Tibbs, and of course his dog, Lenny. However, this home is not without its share of trouble. When the gang wake up one morning to find their home vandalised; bright yellow paint strewn across the wash rooms, in addition to other heinous crimes; Hamish, Tank, Pop, Nutty and their friends must band together to catch the dirty culprit(s).

This a case not without danger; friends fall, grave danger befalls the bravest of heroes, and mistakes cost lives.

Will the cronies responsible for the crimes be caught? Or will the gang members try and fail, their family's lives hanging in the balance...

Characters

Hamish, the leader
Cowboy from the USA
Bobby & Becky twins
Skye
Nutty
Tank – biggest of the caravans
Pop oldest of the caravans

Chapter One
Old Wood

It was October Mr Tibbs was yet again entangled in his tractor engine.

Mr Tibbs lobbed another spanner into the air nearly missing Lenny.

What a dangerous life I lead thought Lenny ducking again to avoid a serious head injury.

Lenny was used to flying spanners; Lenny knew that when all he can see was the back end of those large greasy blue overalls sticking out of the tractor, flying spanners are sure to be expected. Lenny crouched low and rolled casually to his left as another spanner hit the dust narrowly missing his tail.

'Ouch!' said Mr Tibbs. 'I'm sure this darn tractor just bit me,' Mr Tibbs pulled himself out of the engine department, sucking his thumb, cursing and mumbling he headed towards the cottage kitchen in search of the "spanner inflicted first aid kit." Lenny knew exactly where it was next to the veterinary pills, lotions and the funny funnel shaped thing he wore round his neck last summer after the burning tail thing.

Lenny spread out onto the concrete and gave a long sigh a winy whistle followed through his nose - the day was warm for October. The holidaymakers had all gone home. All the caravan awnings dismantled. Squares of brown and yellow grass were left to recover.

Somewhere on the upper fields the large [Hobby continental] stretched his bulky end and forced open his rear window which made a sound much like an uncorked bottle of bubbly producing some gas, 'pardon me,' said Tank raising his head and looking casually about him for some kind of credible response – such as: 'good blow off' or 'descent discharge' or perhaps '10 out of 10.'

Tank looked down at the muddy ground at his side.

'Every year I'm left with this unsightly mush; one would have thought my vast size would be more than enough for those stupid people; without putting up a tent of all things and attaching it to my side.'

Tank spoke as if he was royalty, which was convenient as he often thought he was the king of all the caravans.

Tank the biggest and the moodiest of the hobbies was proud of his wide berth and his super interior design with its island bed, fold down bunks and deluxe bespoke kitchen diner.

"You're not wrong," droned several of the other Hobbies who always agreed with Tank, they were clearly brain washed into believing his superiority was something to be followed and obeyed.

'Of course I'm not wrong,' said Tank. 'Look at the streak marks on my side; unsightly, unnecessary and unremovable! Who's going to clean that off?'

Tank huffed and snorted fussing like a spoilt princess and acting like a big girl's corset or sports bra – which is a bit unfair on large girls who are lovely and cuddly and definitely not fat or ugly.

Just then a small voice could be heard coming from behind the Hobbies somebody was trying to get Tank's attention.

'Excuse me Sir,' the small voice struggled to be heard all the way down the other end of Tank.

Tank opened both front windows as his satellite dish moved full circle to face the small voice standing at the rear end of his bulky frame.

'Excuse me sir I couldn't help hearing you talking about marks on your side and wondered if you would like a wash sir?' said the small voice.

Tank frowned, straining to locate the voice. 'Please address me from the front as directed by my satellite dish, I have some trouble seeing out of my off side rear window which also appears to have some unsightly marks,' said Tank in his best snobby voice.

Tank's satellite dish whirred round slowly the antenna pointy bit twitched as it directed the little girl to the front end of Tanks frame.

The little girl walked along side Tank which took a few minutes and was now facing the front end of Tank, dwarfed by the King of Caravans she wore a bright yellow dress her hair was curly and wild; her face milky with freckles like an ice cream with chocolate dusting. The little girl was swinging a small blue bucket in one hand and holding a large pink sponge in the other and appeared just delightful and cheerful and eager to be helpful.

'How annoying!' said Tank aloud? 'It's a child, what does she think this is a holiday park?' Tank looked at the other Hobbies waiting for an immediate response to his dry humour – none of the other Hobbies picked up on Tanks sarcastic witter.

'Wasted,' said Tank frowning. Tank looked down at the little girl, 'Do you really think that little bucket in your hand is going to hold enough water to wash my supreme 8 berth length?' said Tank with an added grunt.

Tank's front nose picked up high as he glanced around the other Hobbies again looking for response and acknowledgement.

'Just ridiculous!' bellowed Tank his large frame searching from side to side, this time the Hobbies agreed in chorus, "Ridiculous! – Ridiculous!"

They repeated in chorus

"Ridiculous!" until Tank satisfied with level of attention looked away and back towards the little girl – Tanks face was smug his cheeks bulging, mouth closed tight – much like the back end of a hippo's tail bit.

'No of course not sir,' said the little girl casually pointing towards the large length of hose pipe attached to the large brass tap no more than 6 feet away fastened to a bright red post with a sign that said (water station) in large letters.

A sniggering could now be heard amongst the loyal Hobbies, followed by a restrained form of laughter, Tank was not amused. Narrowing his window frames Tank turning to the other Hobbies. 'Something funny you lot'! Tank bellowed.

Back in the mid fields Hamish and the others were discussing who could perform the fastest 360 spin round manoeuvre using some old scaffolding boards on the wet grass, basically a snow board without the snow.

They all knew Cowboy was quickest but Skye wanted to see if he could do better – always the fierce competitor and having seen it on 'Crazy stunt morons' channel 66 – he was sure his technique was a winner.

'Ready – steady- goo!' shouted Hamish.

Cowboy went first he was as fast as any gunslinger from the Wild West – slick – spin and back into position – 'yee haa – whoop whoop!' yelled Cowboy. 'Bit to American and over the top' said Bobby.

'Well done!' Shouted Becky - clapping her window shutters with excitement.

'My turn!' Skye shouted skidding onto the plank and taking off eventually coming full circle and about to spin off again. 'How quick was that then!' he cried still out of control his satellite dish whizzing round and losing all reception.

Hamish jammed his tow bar on top of Skye's front end just in time to stop Skye from tilting backwards and facing the other sky above.

'Well done Skye!' said Becky. 'Not as good as Cowboys,' interrupted Bobby grinning from handle to handle.

'If you can't say anything nice then do not say anything at all,' chirped Becky stabbing a stare at Bobby.

'Oh, how wonderful you both are! What elegance, strength and prowess you display - so breath-taking and... boring!' Bobby shouted.

Summer was all but over and the site was very quiet. Apart from the odd small crisis amongst the older caravans when Pop had lost his tow bar cover and thought he had gone blind when it blew up over his front bay window spectacles.

The brown chocolate colour squares of dark grass where awnings were pinned all summer began their recovery.

The winds picked up; caravans occasionally leaned and swayed like a church choir in harmony and rhythm.

The rains came like a thousand tiny tap dancers opening a Broadway show it was murky buckets again however the weatherman had promised a late summer weekend ahead and Mr Tibbs had plans.

Mr Tibbs could be heard singing above the noise of his tractor mowing the new top field. Lenny was sat in the cab his ears firmly down muffling the awful noise coming from Mr Tibbs not the tractor. It was the last cut of the season Mr Tibbs had been levelling and sowing grass on his new plot all through summer, the wet weather had been good for new growth the large field was now thick and bright with green blades.

Mr Tibbs parked his tractor by the large five-bar gate and jumped down – he lifted his head up and took a deep breath - taking in the sweet smell of the newly cut field and the fresh scented breeze that carried all sorts of delicious perfumes from various wild flowers surrounding the area - Mr Tibbs farted loudly.

'Well Lenny boy – take that in - take it all in!' said Mr Tibbs nodding his head as he surveyed the land around him. Lenny looked hard at Mr Tibbs for a few seconds before turning away with what appeared to be a frown of disapproval.

'Well Lenny boy, it's looking good, this will be a great field for kite flying – football – picnicking and car boot sales.'

Lenny looked up at Mr Tibbs and raised an eyebrow - what about dog walking? Thought Lenny.

Much earlier that day Mr Tibbs had been busy removing a rusty old caravan wreck from the very far end of the field; it had been there a very long time the ground beneath it was dark and dead and needed cultivating.

Mr Tibbs had towed the old caravan down to the lower fields near the woodland out of sight in readiness to be scrapped.

Lenny the ever-watchful camp care taker was again along for the ride bouncing up and down as the tractor trundled along, dragging the old caravan behind. Eventually arriving at the right spot Mr Tibbs performed several manoeuvres eventually positioning the old Caravan in a far corner a little out of site in-between two pines and full on into a gooseberry bush. Lenny looked up and down and scratched his left ear as if to indicate very casually this was the right spot - let's unload.

'It's a miracle this old thing hasn't fallen apart,' said Mr Tibbs as he unhitched the chain from the tow bar. The caravan was filthy with mud and rust.

Mr Tibbs brushed back the nameplate on the front with his muddy hand and read aloud the smudged letters; 'Woodlander 900 - appropriate name, you'll have to stay here for a while Mr Woodlander, until I decide what to do with you, time for a cup of tea Lenny boy and some sprout pie!' Lenny's nose twitched – he did not approve of sprout pie or the after smell of it.

Later that evening the night was drawing in on the Devonshire skyline and the gang deliberated who had scared the most seagulls today.

'This seagull landed on my skylight this morning woke me up,' said Bobby. 'So, I flipped it open real sudden and yelled at him, should have seen him scuttling and flapping.' 'That's cruel!' cried Becky crossly. 'Oh, do me flavour sis,' said Bobby sarcastically making a face.

Hamish yawned loudly; his compartment bonnet opened wide exposing his two front gas bottles. 'I'm bored of bird scare stories we need some action, some adventure – something terrible and frightening and thrilling,' said Hamish.

Cowboy spun round. 'Yeah a real hooting tooting adventure!'

'I'm happy to sit around the site and tell stories,' said Becky.

'Yeah how about a horror story,' Bobby said in a ghoulish voice.

'I've got one!' shouted Hamish, 'this is a good one, gather round boys and girl and listen up.'

Hamish began, 'It was pitch-dark, so dark yea cannie see yer neighbour's tow bar; news had spread of a mad caravan on the loose escaping earlier that day from that place where all the crazy caravans go – (Loony Caravan Park!)' Becky shuffled and began gazing towards the night sky pretended she was not at all interested.

Hamish continued, 'Dark clouds gathered and took the moon, the rain lashed hard like an army of drummers marching into fierce battle, despite hell and fury above everyone on the camp slept soundly as if hypnotised into a deep sleep.'

Becky edged a little closer to Bobby who was already doing the same – they bumped thunderously together, metal on metal.

Hamish looked up sharp and beckoned the others nearer, Hamish cried out, 'Suddenly! - lightning struck the old tree and lit up the sky, there beside the shower block he lay barely visible to the Caravan eye, covered in mud, angry and desperate. The look in his eyes told it all. Crazed with rage ready to inflict terror on any poor unsuspecting caravan that crossed his path!' Hamish kept very still and stared yonder frozen in his final words.

Cowboy sniggered as Bobby and Becky huddled closer together.

'I think I'm going to have an early night,' Skye stammered developing a pretend yawn.

Hamish out of his frozen state raised his voice and croaked at high pitch, 'the young caravan had left the group unawares there was danger nearby!' Skye immediately returned to his original spot. 'I'll stay up a little longer,' he coughed.

Hamish moved in closer to the group now lowering his voice to a barely audible whisper, 'The clap of thunder was so loud no one could hear the screaming.' Hamish took in a breath as if it was his last and held it for at least 10 seconds everyone else appeared to hold their breath in unison.

Just then somewhere in the darkness an unfamiliar voice broke in on the frozen audience. 'Sorry, could you speak up a bit!' The voice had no shape.

The night had camouflaged the muddy figure now sat unseen amongst the group; Bobby and Becky screamed making several thundering bell sounds as they made attempts to huddle tighter together.

'Sorry! I didn't mean to scare you,' piped the voice without body.

'Well you flaming well did,' said Hamish searching the camp trying to make out the muddy shape. 'You scared the life out us!' Hamish growled angrily.

The gang was still tense and trying to focus on the dark space between them. 'How long have you been there?' said Skye trying to sound brave, his voice a little shaky and high pitched?

The murky shape barely visible quivered and moved like a large chocolate jelly. 'About 10 minutes', said the voice. 'I didn't want to interrupt the story, it really was very good.'

'Never mind the story you gave us all a battery attack, anyway who the hell are you?' Hamish demanded. 'Sorry I'm Woodlander – the names Nutty.'

'Got that right,' said Bobby. 'Don't be rude,' said Becky nudging Bobby hard.

'Where have you come from Nutty?' asked Becky politely.

'I'm from the big field on the upper level. It's been neglected for years, I've been left in the corner near the trees, I'm afraid I've got a bit dirty over time.'

'That's the field Mr Tibbs has been cultivating all summer,' said Cowboy. 'That's right, said Nutty.' Mr Tibbs bought the land at auction, it used to belong to old Mrs Drake she died a couple of years ago; Mr Tibbs towed me down to the lower fields earlier today and left me near the woods.'

'Well Mr scary Woodlander - meet the gang,' said Hamish introducing everyone.

'We'll get you cleaned up in the morning see what colour you really are.'

'I'd appreciate that, it's really nice to meet you all, sorry I scared you.'

'I wasn't scared,' said Bobby pushing his chest out.

'Yeah right,' said Cowboy. 'That's why your hub caps have fallen off and your water barrels empty.'

Chapter Two
Damage Done

Like all good farmers or campsite owners Mr Tibbs was up early.

'Lots to do today - Lenny boy!' Said Mr Tibbs joyfully.

'Goanna paint the shower block this afternoon; now where did I put those brushes?'

Lenny raised his eyebrows and thought, why ask me - do I look like a decorator.

Mr Tibbs wagged his finger at each item in his trailer mumbling out loud the list in his head: 'Paint ... brushes ... rollers ...ladders.'

The old tractor trundled up the concrete path shaking and bouncing the trailer behind. Paint pots and brushes danced together changing position as they jumped up and down like keen rock and rollers. Lenny kept an eye on the contents from the back of the tractor, barking if anything tried to escape.

Mr Tibbs pulled up at the top of the hill just outside the shower block.

Paint tins in hand and under arms, a large paintbrush between his teeth Mr Tibbs was armed for decorative assault.

Suddenly Mr Tibbs stopped in his tracks like an obedient soldier called to halt. His mouth dropped open the paintbrush released between his teeth dropped onto Lenny's head.

'What the darn diggins!' Mr Tibbs yelled at his shower block.

The scene was carnage. The shower block had been vandalised.

Windows were broken, sink units ripped off, signs torn down but worst of all painted across the front in large yellow letters:

'HOLLY TRASH SITE*'*

Mr Tibbs was furious; removing his cap he threw it hard at the ground, Lenny barked at the hat not really sure if it was the cause of Mr Tibbs anger but remained vigilant and on guard.

Cowboy came skidding down the hill. 'Hey, you guys, something's happened to the upper hillside shower block,' he hollered.

'What's happened?' said Hamish.

'Someone has vandalised the block, broken the windows, busted the sinks and painted *Holly trash site* all over in bright yella paint,' said Cowboy in Wild West style.

'Look better in green,' said Bobby. 'Shut up Bobby,' said Becky frowning. 'That's awful,' Becky gave Bobby a firm stare.

'Let's take a look, come on you lot,' said Hamish pacing on up the hill. The gang followed their leader.

'Wow what a mess someone really doesn't like our caravan site,' said Skye shaking his front end.

'But who would do such a thing? 'It's not like Mr Tibbs has any enemies,' Becky said appealing for suggestions.

'What's up?' said a familiar voice. The shady green caravan sat casually between Cowboy and Skye surveying the wreck that was once the shower block.

'Nutty isn't it?' said Hamish looking curious at the green caravan. 'You sure like sneaking up on us Mr Nutty Woodlander,' Hamish continued to fix his stare at Nutty.

'Sorry about that,' said Nutty. 'You had a wash?' said Becky inquisitively.

'You look different although still sort of camouflaged; you've gone from forest brown to grassy green.'

'Yeah conveniently unseen!' said Bobby looking round at the others for agreement.

'Yeah one of the Traveller children offered to clean me up this morning; I almost forgot what colour I was, it took hours,' Nutty smiled.

'Yes, the Romany travellers are back on the site, they come every year,' said Hamish releasing his firm stare.

'You don't think they had anything to do with this?' Nutty suggested looking around at the carnage.

'We don't point the blame at people we know well,' said Skye defensively.

'It's the ones we don't know,' said Bobby staring at Nutty.

'We don't know anything!' said Becky looking at Hamish for approval.

'Well it's not good,' said Hamish. 'We need to come up with a plan, we need to find out who did this, it's our site and were not having this, are we?' Hamish had that authoritative tone to his voice.

'Darn right, let's find them; shoot them down, string 'em up!' Cowboy said dancing around pretending he had pistols on his doors.

'So, what is the plan Hamish?' said Skye.

'Yeah, how are we going to find out who has done this?' Bobby said still looking at Nutty.

'Not sure,' said Hamish. 'I may have to get some advice; I'm going to see Pop.' Hamish made his way to the lower fields.

Pop and the senior caravans had already heard of the damage to the shower block. 'Can't understand it, who would do such a thing? We're such a quiet site.' Pop looked yonder a cross to the hills towards the woods: 'Nearly 2,000 trees I know every one of them, every narrow road, hedge line and hump back bridge for 50 miles. Used to be alert, had my Ariel up high, knew what was going on; these damn satellite dishes pick up 100 channels but can't tell me what's going on in my own back yard!'

'Hello Pop, Permission to come aboard sir?' Said Hamish, knowing Pop liked any reference to pop's Sea faring days on and off the ferry boats at Dover and Calais.

'Hello young Hamish, permission granted son; I gather you've come about the mysterious damage to our site?'

'Yes sir,' Hamish found himself standing to attention.

'At ease son, I've heard all about it: senseless damage, no obvious reason, no clues, no tracks, yep It's a mystery son.'

Pop paced for a while, Hamish kept quiet he knew Pop was thinking and waited respectfully.

'Well!' Pop said loudly and tripping up as he turned quickly. 'Darn uneven ground round here,' Pop gained his balance.

Hamish raised his shutters high in expectation standing to attention and awaiting orders.

'It maybe a mystery, however there must a reason, some devil has a gripe with our site and we need to find out who before more damage is done!' Pop sounded like a Prime Minister preparing for war, raising his front-end high and waving his antenna. 'We need a plan Hamish lad, whoever is doing this doesn't want to be seen and is using the cover of darkness to carry out the damage, darn rogue must be caught.'

'What can we do Pop?' said Hamish keen and eager.

'Hamish lad, to catch a rogue, you have to think like one!' Pop beckoned Hamish closer his voice lowered to a whisper.

'Question son, if you were intent on doing more damage to our site, what would you do next?' Pop backed off and closed his front window waiting for Hamish to reply.

Hamish narrowed his front shutters, his satellite dish moved slowly around like a second hand on a watch face.

Hamish began to nod excitingly agreeing with his thoughts, Hamish spoke with caution looking at Pop intensely to check each word was right and then speeding up his answer. 'Damage – the – other- shower block on the lower fields its right by the woods and easy to approach unseen!' Hamish cried out a little over excited.

'Shush!' Pop looked around cautiously. 'We don't know who's about young Hamish, and yes your right lad – I was a bit of a rogue in my day and that's what I would do.'

Hamish looked a little puzzled at Pop. 'What are you staring at lad,' said Pop frowning. 'Nothing,' said Hamish. 'Right,' said Pop. Now pay attention.'

'So, the plan is you and your friends need to hide out near the second shower block - watch and wait for our vandal and catch him red handed, nail the son of bitch to the wall!' Pop screwed his face up and looked proper mean.

Hamish stared at Pop a little surprised. 'Yes sir,' he stammered. 'We'll nail his ... and catch him by the ... Hamish saluted and left Pop grimacing and a little red in the face.

Chapter Three
Hide and Seek

Later that night the gang took turns hiding in pairs close to the woods near the giant Oak. They had borrowed a large weather cover from the Hobbies, big enough to cover two of the gang huddled together. The cover was green and brown ideal camouflage for spying and giving the appearance of a very large bolder.

Three nights had passed: It was Bobby and Becky's turn to keep watch.

'Did you hear something?' Bobby whispered.

'No – stop saying that, it's just the wind, move over a bit.' Becky said shunting Bobby. 'What time is it?' said Bobby.

'Time you shut up,' Becky said crossly. 'We are supposed to be under cover; I know we're twins but I don't want to be this close to you for any occasion.

Nine months of manufacture was enough,' Becky grunted and closed her shutters.

'Hey,' said Bobby whispering. 'What?' Becky huffed raising one shutter.

'We are under cover – under… cover,' Bobby repeated slowly. 'Get it?'

Becky sighed, shaking her head slowly and looking up, 'why me? Is it not bad enough we are related?' Several hours had past - the camouflage sheet lay still, except for a very slight gentle rise – up and down - accompanied by synchronised snoring.

The sun pierced through the gaps in the cover. The full brightness of the morning woke Bobby and Becky as Hamish and the gang pulled the cover off their backs.

It wasn't just the yellow colour of the sun that faced them in all its glory.

In large dripping letters; across the front porch of the now broken shower block the words:

'Idiots caravan site'

'Oh, no!' Cried Becky closing her shutters abruptly and opening them again very slowly, hoping the written words were just the flash back of a bad dream.

'You two are useless!' said Skye crossly. 'Darn it, three nights we've been waiting for those slickers,' Cowboy pretended to throw a hat to the ground in dramatic frustration, just like the in the movies.

'OK everyone, let's just calm down, it's not easy staying up all night,' said Hamish feeling sorry for Becky. 'Whoever did this must have been really sneaky – look the door is missing,' Hamish moved closer to the shower block.

'That must have taken some time to unscrew the hinges and remove the whole door,' said Skye.

Hamish had a good look around, he frowned, and his satellite began to move slowly from side to side as if he were scanning the area waiting to pick up a signal or a clue.

'Have you found a trail boss?' said Cowboy eagerly.

'We didn't hear a thing last night,' said Bobby.

'Some lookout you are,' said Skye frowning.

'We stayed up as late as we could!' Becky's voice began to crack as she held back the tears.

'Leave my sister alone!' demanded Bobby, springing to Becky's defence.

Hamish was busy scanning the ground for clues. 'Be quiet you lot!' 'I think I've found something.'

Hamish tilted low. 'It's a foot print – a yellow print.'

Just visible at the end of the shower block, clearly marked in yellow paint the heel of a boot could be seen. The track marks continued through the grass leading a way to the side of the building followed by knee high streaks of yellow marks brushed through onto the lengthy grass.

'Look!' Said Skye, 'there's a crease running through the grass towards the woods that must be where they dragged the door off.' Skye started off quickly down the newly found track.

'Whoa there!' shouted Cowboy, 'that track narrows just up by the river you won't get through - the pass is closed.'

'We'll have to go round the outside and up the hedge road,' suggested Bobby.

The gang convoyed up the small narrow lane at the back of the woods.

The sun flashed between the trees bouncing off the river; shafts of golden light hurled themselves through the gaps as if helping the gang to search the bank.

'I see something!' shouted Cowboy pulling up suddenly.

The rest of the gang piled up behind Cowboy, tow bars colliding – metal on metal – clank!

'Ouch!' could have warned us you were going to stop so suddenly,' Becky frowned nursing her front end.

'Look yonder on the far bank you can see it,' Cowboy pointed with his dish.

Lying on the opposite riverbank was the shower block door.

'Whoever did this must have used the door like some kind of raft,' said Cowboy catching his breath.

Hamish moved closer to the trees for a better look. 'I, it looks that way, but why such a dramatic escape from the scene of the crime?'

'Something must have disturbed them! Bobby shouted, must have been me and Becky I thought I heard something during the night, I knew I wasn't dreaming.'

'Yeah they heard something… snoring,' said Skye chuckling.

'Shush!' said Hamish. The gang silenced immediately:

Cowboy tensed, Bobby moved in front of Becky, Skye pushed out his front bay and stood proud next to Hamish.

The gang could hear rustling from the other side of the bank. Something or someone was coming through the bush.

'What should we do?' Skye whispered to Hamish not moving an inch.

Hamish was thinking hard; his satellite dish began spinning.

'I'm going to head for that gap between the trees, there's just enough room and the waters shallow at that turn in the river.' Hamish stiffened and readied himself.

The river was shallow in places more of a large stream during the dry season.

The gap in the trees was a fisherman's spot no bushes or long grass, the bank was low and just a short drop.

Hamish whispered: 'If I take off from that area, I should make it at least half way a cross in one effort; the riverbed is mostly shingle stone that will give my wheels enough grip to launch me the rest of the way taking them by surprise.'

The sun appeared to bow out just as Hamish moved into position. A slight breeze moved through the trees, the atmosphere changed it felt like something ghostly. As the wind picked up the newly fallen leaves ran towards the gang like a surging crowd, something was happening.

Hamish steadied himself his wheels backed up slowly - a half turn, the gang watched from the bank intensely.

Hamish shouted out a full Scottish war cry – 'Come on yoooooz!' taking a big breath he was just about to launch himself off the riverbank towards the other side.

Hamish halted suddenly almost as dramatic as he took off, nearly tipping up onto his roof.

From a cross the bank for all to see there was quite a spectacle – an unexpected spectacle. In-between every bush little heads emerged - colourful, like flowers popping up for spring - with the most delightful smiles - stood not one, but at least ten - small children, mostly girls.

They were all a similar age - about eight or maybe 10. Their smiles became brighter, beaming and radiant like the sun that appeared as if on cue lighting up the moment.

The gang stood silent and could not help but too slowly - smile back a little awkwardly and with much surprise.

Chapter Four
Fix It Up

The children on the other side of the river bank stood out bright and colourful. Their clothes were handmade - all had large shiny buttons on their fronts like colourful sweets from a jar.

One girl stood out from the rest, her hair was chestnut brown a mass of curls like candyfloss, her beautiful locks held together with a peach ribbon that waved gloriously in the breeze like a ships flag.

'Hello!' the candyfloss girl called over, backed up by a cheerful repeat chorus of 'hello!' from all the other girls and boys.

'Crikey' said Hamish. 'Hello! Hamish shouted back across the bank, still steadying himself from his attempted take off, his tow bar now covered in mud and rapped with nettles.

The girl called back: 'my name is Ruby these are my cousins we are on the lower field we heard about the damage to the shower block and wondered if we could help?'

Hamish smiled awkwardly and looked at the others- for once Hamish appeared lost for words.

'Thank you, that's very good of you, I'm not sure what you can do though?' Hamish shouted across the river.

'We can all paint and some of the boys know basic fixing stuff because they've watched the elders at work, Ruby smiled broadly and turned to her cousins, who all nodded.

Hamish began to nod back parrot fashion – 'Okay that's great!' said Hamish still nodding – the gang gave Hamish a long look – 'what?' said Hamish starting off.

'OK everyone' said Ruby – 'let's carry this door back through the wood!'
The children each found a place around the door and lifted it high

above their heads; all of them being a similar height this worked well and off they went through the bushes like little soldier ants carrying off their nesting.

Back at the site Mr Tibbs had now discovered the damage to the second shower block.

Mr Tibbs was near to retirement and in his late fifties, the years had been kind to him, he had a young face, browned from being outdoors all his life; he had a Mediterranean look.

However today Mr Tibbs looked older than his years, beaten down with anger and worry - Mr Tibbs was not a happy man.

'What have I done Lenny?' Mr Tibbs removed his hat and scratched his thick dark hair. He looked down at Lenny his eyes a little glazed.

'Who wants to ruin my business and scupper my retirement?' 'Have we got enemies Lenny boy?'

Lenny looked back into Mr Tibbs sad glassy eyes, he knew his master was upset and he barked to acknowledge his friends despair and at the hat which Lenny now suspected was the culprit.

Lenny was a brave dog and clever he liked approval and continued barking at the shower block as if to say: If you're still in there you better come out and face me right now!

Mr Tibbs flipped his hat back on his head and blew hard and long, letting out a short whistle as his lips pursed together.

Lenny's ears perked up and his tail wagged responding to his master's high pitch signal.

'Come on Lenny, we need to find some tools and put our thinking caps on.'

Later that day Becky and Bobby were dozing back to back their snoring almost in sync, like a couple of old lawn mowers revving up and down as they slept soundly.

Cowboy was acting out some kind of shoot out near the trees, muttering words like: 'Take that!' - 'Gotcha!' - 'thought you were fast ha!'

– 'don't mess with the best!'

Skye and Hamish were sat quietly together. Skye looked up to Hamish like an older brother they had a lot in common. Hamish was a natural leader: brave, level headed, calm and strong willed. Skye was eager to learn, sometimes too eager but with good intentions.

Hamish had spent his early years in Glasgow Scotland, mainly laid up in the caravan show parks. Hamish also spent some time in the highlands getting used to the wet summers and ice-cold winters; before being driven down to the warm south coast.

Skye came from Newcastle and spent his early years near the River Tyne just by the Tyne Bridge; the best Fishing River in the North of England for Salmon and Trout.

Skye knew about the rivers and had always loved the sound of running water.

Skye emerged from his thoughts. 'Seems strange that the door was used as a raft to make their escape,' he said looking at Hamish for an answer, 'the river has too many shallow spots, and it was never going to take them far?'

Hamish was thinking hard. 'I - perhaps they deliberately placed the door into the river to make it look like they came from far away,' said Hamish thinking even harder his satellite now spinning and humming.

'You mean it maybe someone closer to home!' Skye frowned, copying Hamish's expression – he sighed.

Hamish looked far across the fields in search of inspiration.

The high hills were shaped like a school of Humpback whales, sheep lay in huddles like small balls of cotton, trees dotted between them like splashes of green and the grass changed colour with the passing shade from gold to orange.

Just then a clear yet small voice interrupted and pulled the pair from their thoughts.

'Would you like to help us?' said the cheerful voice her hair still bouncing from her run from the lower fields.

Ruby was bobbing around, skipping and jumping like she had springs in her boots. 'We have tools and paint, some of us have started and the boys kind of know what to do with the plumbing but would like some guidance.'

'I know about water and stuff,' said Skye, 'How about if I'm project manager?'

'Fine, whatever that is, it sounds great,' said Ruby beaming as she bounced off towards the shower block. 'See you there!' she shouted.

Later at the shower block the children were chatting and arguing, trying to sort out who was a painter and who was a plumber. Everyone wanted to do something to help.

'OK now listen up!' said Skye in his best authoritative voice.

'Who wants to paint?'

All the girls put their hands up. A chorus of colour ideas erupted.

'Yellow! – Pink! – Orange! – Green! – Red! – Purple! – Blue!'

'Hang on; we need to keep the block the same colour or something neutral!' said Skye looking back discreetly at Hamish. 'I heard that on the TV on one of those DIY programmes,' Skye winked.

Becky had also been invited and was team leading the girls, 'Right girls let's paint this block as pretty as a rainbow!'

'Becky!' Skye yelped.

Becky smiled broadly as she danced passed Skye with a mischievous look in her eye. 'You project manage the boys and I will manage the girls,' right girls? The girls cheered with a few whoops and hollers.

Hamish smiled and looked at Skye raising his shutters.

'Go to it project leader!' said Hamish shaking his head, barely containing his laughter.

The boys were busy arguing over what tools to use and the best wrench to dismantle the twisted pipe work around the sinks.

'We need flexible rods!' - 'Slip joint pliers!' – 'Copper gaskets!' – 'Compression joints!' – 'Isolation valves!' - 'Adjustable spanner!'

One of the boys over eager to start the repairs accidentally pulled off a main pipe from beneath the battered sink unit.

A jet of high-powered water hit Skye full in the windows and spun him round soaking his back end too.

Skye struggled to move out of the way, the loose pipe had a will of its own and appeared to follow Skye's every move like a well-trained marks man – everywhere Skye moved the jet of water followed him.

Hamish was now hysterical with laughter. 'You'll make a great highland dancer!' he shouted.

Skye was jigging and bouncing around, back and forth, trying to dodge the jet of water. One of the boys eventually found the stopcock at the side of the block and turned the water off.

Skye sat dripping and gleaming, streaks running down from every window.

The sun came out in sympathy to dry Skye out, adding to the fun and laughter.

Cowboy and Bobby came up the hill to see what all the fuss and hollering was about.

'Why are you wetter than the Mississippi River?' said Cowboy.

'About time you had a wash,' said Bobby grinning.

Skye had no choice but to laugh.

Much later that day Mr Tibbs and Lenny came jigging and bouncing up the hill in the old tractor.

The old girl chugged and chatted as it pulled the trailer, like an old steam train smoke popping and banging from the upward pipe.

Lenny's head was nodding freely up and down, his eyes jostling from side to side as if trying to say, 'Can you please keep my head still.'

Mr Tibbs was looking tired and sad; his cap was lower than usual hiding his face from the work to be done and the disappointment of the whole day.

Mr Tibbs pulled up near the block; hand braked the tractor and jumped down; he paused for a moment mustering the energy he didn't have.

Lenny barked and whined.

Mr Tibbs wasn't taking any notice, he sighed and groaned, lost in his thoughts as he began to unload the trailer, listing the contents out loud: 'Paint, tool bag, brush, dustpan, darn it I've forgotten my shovel!'

Lenny barked again.

Mr Tibbs kicked the trailer wheel hard and turned sharply towards

Lenny.

'Will you shut – up – Lenny?' Mr Tibbs was struck silent his mouth opened wide like an obedient patient at the dentist.

The shower block was different, much different.

Mr Tibbs thought he was seeing things, bold colours of red and black stood out a bright yellow pattern surrounded the windows. There were pretty flower designs in between the sinks, purples, and pinks with bright green leaves and trailing stems leading to lacy designs of swirls and circles that danced around the windows and skirting.

All the sinks were straight, secured and perfectly in line
shining bright like soldier's helmets ready to do battle.

The block had been transformed, looking not unlike a classic traveller's caravan, traditional, colourful, smart and artistic.

'Well slap me with a kipper!' Mr Tibbs removed his cap slapping his knee with it. 'Will you look at that Lenny?'

Lenny barked and wagged his tail in approval.

Chapter Five
Close Encounter

Mr Tibbs rumbled into his courtyard with Lenny in the trailer eager to jump out.

Mr Tibbs was whistling one of his high-pitched tunes that made Lenny cringe.

'I don't know who's been helping us repair the block and I'm not too sure about the new decoration, but I suppose it's kind of different, aye, Lenny boy!'

Mr Tibbs always talked aloud to Lenny. Lenny was good company and had been with Mr Tibbs since he was a puppy. Mr Tibbs never married and had lived on the farm all his life, content with the company of animals and the holidaymakers who came every year.

Mr Tibbs entered the cottage throwing his cap on the old pine dresser narrowly missing his collection of prized cups for the village sprout growing competition – fifth in a row at the village fate. Mr Tibbs kept his boots on - the old quarry floor was already thick with dried mud Mr Tibbs was not house proud.

Lenny did his usual 360-degree turn and sat snugly on the old fleece near the pantry. Lenny loved to smell the cheese wafting through the gaps in the pantry door, filtering through his nose, although Lenny didn't like the taste of cheese and always rejected it when Mr Tibbs offered a small portion. Although he preferred it to sprout soup with that strange after smell that always appeared after Mr Tibbs had eaten.

Mr Tibbs lit up the old stove and placed the kettle on the burner, Lenny's ear perked up as it always did when Mr Tibbs put the kettle on.

Lenny loved a saucer of tea; 'I'm sure you were a cat in a previous life Lenny boy.'

No, thought Lenny, I was never a cat I like chasing birds not eating them.

Mr Tibbs sank into the old leather chair that always creaked and groaned and made other noises when he slept. 'Sounds how I feel, this old chair,' said Mr Tibbs. Lenny looked up; you always say that he thought.

Mr Tibbs was tapping his half-empty mug with his grubby forefinger. Lenny was now at his master's feet eyeing the mug and doing his best glassy eye expression, his tongue now hanging from his mouth desperate and dry.

Mr Tibbs looked up and down, his head turned to the left and then to the right, in every direction except at Lenny's thirsty tongue.

Lenny's head turned to the side; there was serious thinking going on Mr Tibbs sat up suddenly, Lenny hopped backward and raise a paw as if to say - yes, you've remembered to give me some tea, let's have it then you silly old fart!

'It's great that somebody is helping to fix the shower block, we're not completely surrounded by enemies but this will not stop, we need to do some detective work Lenny boy!'

Mr Tibbs emptied his mug in the sink and looked out of the window across the yard towards the woods. Lenny was looking at the sink wondering what happened to his tea.

'We're going to have a good look around Lenny, see if we can find some clues in those woods, it's the only place where someone could hide before vandalising the shower block.'

Mr Tibbs slapped his cap back on his wiry hair and gave a slap to his thigh that signalled to Lenny – let's go.

Outside Mr Tibbs unhitched the trailer from his tractor, Lenny jumped up to share the large cast metal seat that was loosely covered with an old flattened cushion, just enough room for one large bottomed farmer and small discoloured hound.

They headed towards the woods. Mr Tibbs had a determined look on his face, with his faithful sidekick; *Detective* Tibbs and *Sergeant* Lenny were after some bad guys.

The woods were dense and still thick with greenery; the autumn air was still warm only a few trees had begun the change. Fresh green still outnumbered gold and brown.

Pathways were ever changing, walkers and horse riders forcing new ground; a labyrinth of short grasses and muddy hills crossed and turned mapping the area.

It was late afternoon the sun was still finishing its day, patches of light cast shadows. Shapes appeared and disappeared as shade and light moved across the barks and foliage nothing really appeared to move.

Mr Tibbs and Lenny were cutting a wary pace through the thickest part of the woods. 'Looking for tracks' Mr Tibbs said under his breath his head swaying from side to side.

Lenny looked up in agreement and copied his master's movements, his nose twitching, flooded with scent.

The pair came to a clearing, the sun had all but retired for the day and a grey mass above threatened rain.

Ivy and nettles spread across wiry bark a small number of wild flowers still holding on to colour keeping their heads high. In the middle of the clearing lay a huge fallen tree inviting all to sit for a while and consider the next trail?

Snake pathways lay in all directions; Lenny scrambled onto the log and stretched his neck high taking in the now damp air.

Mr Tibbs also took the fallen tree's invitation and sat awkwardly struggling for a while to gain some comfort, his boots slipping on the greasy green bark.

The surrounding trees began to dance gently as a breeze passed through signalling rain.

Mr Tibbs didn't mind the rain, well weathered himself his tough skin was practically waterproof.

Lenny didn't like the rain; he shook his body and puffed his fur out looking around for cover.

'Let's move on Lenny boy,' said Mr Tibbs attempting to jump clear of the log and losing his footing; Mr Tibbs slipped backwards unable to catch himself inevitably ended on the other side of the log flat on his back; fortunately, he landed on something thick and dry and soft.

Lenny barked. 'I'm alright - I'm alright' repeated Mr Tibbs as he struggled to his feet, Mr Tibbs looked down at what had cushioned his fall, it was a large thick brown coat, with dirty white woolly lining.

'What have we got here?' Mr Tibbs held the coat up high and looked it up and down, Lenny barked again.

The coat wasn't entirely brown in colour. 'Well will you look at that Lenny!'

Clearly visible on the right sleeve were splashes of yellow – yellow paint.

Mr Tibbs placed the coat on the log and spread it out. 'This belongs to a big chap over six feet tall with long arms; this belongs to the villain who wrecked our shower block!' Mr Tibbs frowned as he searched thoroughly through the pockets.

Mr Tibbs angrily poked and patted the coat almost as if the villain were still in it. Suddenly, the coat gave up a hidden secret. Out fell an object. Mr Tibbs followed it as it fell, and he bent down and picked up a penknife.

The knife was clearly old about four inches long it was made of some kind of ivory. Mr Tibbs examined it closely.

'Nice piece of work,' he said. Mr Tibbs turned it around and upside down, examining it closely like a jeweller surveying a rare diamond.

His poor eyesight finally adjusting, the picture on the handle became clear to Mr Tibbs. It was a very detailed carving of a caravan, a traveller caravan, and in the corner, some one's initials – B.D.

Time stood still in the woods, seconds seemed like hours. Just then silence broke; from the East Side of the clearing the faint sound of barking could be heard. Mr Tibbs woke from staring at the knife and looked sharply towards the interruption. 'Someone's come back for their coat,' said Mr Tibbs scowling.

Nothing could be seen from where they were standing, Lenny was alert and looked keen at his master for instructions.

Mr Tibbs looked down at Lenny and Lenny took this as a signal, - he was off like a racehorse from the stocks.

Lenny's little legs hardly touching the ground as he bounded off through the rough ground; dodging and weaving eventually out of site heading towards the unknown.

'Darn it Lenny!' Mr Tibbs began to take chase but his knees had other ideas as he hopped with pain, the old joints needed warming up first before a cross-country race.

'Lenny! – Lenny! – Here boy! Mr Tibbs shouted as he reached the East Side.

Mr Tibbs picked up pace through some prickly bracken. Not entirely sure where he was going Mr Tibbs followed an old trail dragging back hanging branches and kicking through nettle thundering through like a charging rhino in the jungle. Sweat now shining on his forehead Mr Tibbs still had hold of the coat, it was heavy, and the knife was still tight in his hand.

'Lenny! That darn dog.' suddenly a high-pitched yelp rang out cutting the silence like a chainsaw; Mr Tibbs froze and looked sharp across as several wood pigeons took flight from a silver birch.

Mr Tibbs took up pace he forgot about the pain in his knees as he hurried to the source of the cry, his teeth gritted he held the coat and the knife tighter, fisting both hands as he ran hard.

At a relentless pace Mr Tibbs broke through a large bush, past the silver birch and past Lenny, who lay dirty - bloody and quiet – in the thick bracken of ferns.

It was getting dark and the rain soaked everything, the last dregs of light only favoured the pale and less dense, Mr Tibbs shouted again for the umpteenth time – Lenny…!'

Chapter Six
Confession

'Well of course it's not my idea of a makeover,' said Tank boasting to the other Hobbies. 'Battle ship grey would have been a far more suitable colour for a shower block, no silly frilly colours and patterns, after all it's just a toilet.' The other Hobbies as always – agreed with Tank.

Becky over hearing Tank's frank opinion broke in, with a stern reply, 'I think we did a really good job and your opinion is not welcome!

And another thing,' said Becky crossly, 'you're a stuffy, loud mouth, rude…'

Hamish shunted Becky away and forced a smile at Tank, 'We are all entitled to our opinions, battle ship grey can be a very effective colour on commercial buildings' said Hamish holding an uncomfortable smile.

Tank raised an eyebrow at Hamish and shot a stare at Becky.

'He's an old battle ship,' said Bobby - quietly defending his sister.

'Shut up you two,' said Hamish, still aware of Tanks presence.

Just then Cowboy and Skye came steaming up the hill followed by Nutty Woodlander several caravan spaces behind. 'I win!' puffed Skye.

'Yeah only because I let you partner,' Cowboy spun round facing the hill. 'Come on slow coach!' he shouted back at Nutty.

'Sorry guys!' replied Nutty, 'I'm not much of sportsman, I'm so unfit, my under-carriage is rattling and my hinges are loose!'

'Ha Excuses!' shouted Cowboy.

Cowboy took a rested position, lowering his frame and catching his breath. Cowboy sat beaming broadly at Nutty still struggling up the hill.

'That's funny,' said Cowboy adjusting his view.

'What's funny?' Hamish looked at Cowboy and then followed his stare towards Nutty.

'Yellow and green,' said Cowboy.

'What are you talking about?' said Skye joining in.

'Nutty's undercarriage - it has streaks of yellow all over it, look,' said Cowboy.

They all stared as Nutty struggled up the hill. Under his green coloured body yellow streaks stood out clearly on his under carriage visible from the 45% angle as he came up the hill.

Nutty arrived at the top of hill; catching his breath he was unaware of the silence and the hard-faced reception that met him.

'Wow that was great fun, it's been a long time since I've raced like that, you're too fast for me Cowboy,' said Nutty blowing hard.

Hamish stepped forward, as the others moved in closer; Cowboy stood next to Hamish who now had a stern look to his bay window, his shutters lowered to a frown.

Cowboy spoke first. 'You're yellow,' Cowboy said coldly.

Nutty laughed, 'yeah right Cowboy, we gonna have a shootout, nobody calls me yella.'

Nutty side-stepped and pretended to draw and fire.

Hamish spoke out firmly. 'What Cowboy means is that you have yellow paint streaks on your undercarriage, we could see them as you came up the hill and we'd like to know how you came to have them?' Hamish looked at Nutty with his most serious expression.

Nutty's light-hearted gunslinger impression evaporated, he finally noticed that no one was joking, his face dropped and his eyes moved from side to side, he looked frustrated and suspicious.

'I don't... know... what... You're talking about!' spluttered Nutty, his voice tone was not convincing.

'There must be some explanation?' said Becky.

'Yeah come on Mr Nutty Woodlander,' Bobby demanded.

'I always thought there was something not quite right about you.'

'Don't be so rude Bobby, I'm sure Nutty has a reasonable explanation,' Becky looked at Nutty hopefully.

Nutty now looked very nervous. 'I have nothing to hide, you must be confused, it's probably the Sun's glare bouncing off my hub caps,' Nutty began moving slowly backwards.

'I have to go now … I need to take a nap … I'm really tired after that race.'

Suddenly before his wheels took another turn, Nutty found himself wedged solid between two very large caravans; Nutty had been gripped tightly between Tank and another Hobby who were listening nearby.

'Well then, my friend,' said Tank casually, 'We'll take a good look at your undercarriage to make sure were not all just seeing reflections of sun light or perhaps you've just laid too long in the buttercup field!'

Before Nutty could utter another word, he found himself rising up between the giant Hobbies as they pushed together forcing Nutty's small oval frame to be squeezed and pushed high off the ground.

'Going up, first floor!' said Tank grinning.

'Put me down!' cried Nutty.

'You have no right to treat me like this!' he squirmed.

Nutty was now at least 10 feet off the ground, looking much like a part of some kind of acrobatic act, although his expression was not that of a confident daredevil circus performer more of a frightened cat up a tree.

From this elevated view, the gang could clearly see several streaks of yellow paint covering different areas of Nutty's undercarriage; the evidence was clear as paint.

'I can explain!' Nutty hollered from above.

'Before you say another word!' said Hamish cutting in with a very clear authoritative voice, 'listen very carefully my friend!'

'The more you say Mr Woodlander, the guiltier you appear … the more you say … the more likely you are to say something foolish … however your silence will only make us think that you are guilty of something!'

'I can explain!' yelled Nutty.

Hamish interrupted Nutty's pleading once more. 'Mr Woodlander before you speak, you need to be very honest with us … if you choose to feed us with lame excuses and adventurous fables … we will be forced to deal with you in an adventurous way only fit for liars and spies!'

Hamish continued. 'Unless you think you are highly intelligent and imaginative, you might want to take into consideration before you speak the possible circumstances … twists of fate … and your current position, especially as you are so far upward and so close to a very steep hill!'

'Wow, you sound really scary, like an Italian Mafia gangster,' whispered Cowboy leaning into Hamish.

'Glaswegian crime lord actually,' whispered Hamish, raising an eyebrow.

'OK, put me down I confess, I'll tell you everything. I'm not messing with you guys; give me a chance to speak please!' Nutty spluttered.

Only after a signal from Hamish the Hobbies lowered the nervous looking Nutty down and stood guard only inches away.

'Thank you, Tank,' said Hamish looking hard at Nutty. 'Let's hear it then?'

Nutty began to tell the story:

'During my time in the upper field ... the one that used to belong to Miss Drake. A farmer named Fingle and some of his workers from the North Star farm on the far side ... used me to hideout in when they were planning poaching and illegal fishing on Miss Drakes land.'

Nutty continued: 'One night I heard the men talking about buying the field ... which would give them direct access to the river and the woods.'

'When Miss Drake died last year, the field came up for auction. Fingle was out bid for the sale by your Mr Tibbs.

'Mr Fingle was furious and came up with a plan to ruin Mr Tibbs Park; they would continue to use me when I was moved down into the lower field close to woods ... it was easy to hide and store the paint used to vandalise the shower blocks.'

Nutty finished his story.

'I was perfect cover ... wait until dark ... allowing them to move quickly ... doing the damage and then hiding in me until it was clear.'

'It all makes sense now why didn't you tell us!' said Becky angrily. 'I thought we were your friends?'

'I know I've been a fool, I heard them talk of re painting me and placing me back in the top field so they could continue using me for a base for fishing and shooting.'

'I've been incredibly stupid, I'm ashamed, I should have told you guys, I was thinking of myself its typical of my life ... I deserve to rot a way in the swamp.'

'No good feeling sorry for yourself!' said Becky crossly, everyone has weaknesses and insecurities; some of us aren't as strong as others and haven't got friends to support us. We are willing to support you and give you our friendship if you can prove to us that you deserve it!'

'Hang on a minute - we can't trust him, after all the lies!' cried Skye.

'No - Becky's right,' Hamish looked sternly at everyone. 'We will give you a chance Mr Woodlander, however be warned - you are being watched.'

Tank interrupted. 'Good God, what a soft bunch you are, I was quite happy to play caravan bowls with our dishonest friend here…fools,' said Tank as he strode off with the other Hobbies repeating after him – 'fools!'

'Thank you … Tank!' Hamish called out as the Hobbies marched off like a giant Brontosaurus herd.

Chapter Seven
Confrontation

Mr Tibbs took the pan of hot milk off the stove and knelt down near the fireplace. He poured the milk gently into a bowl with the cute kitten picture on it that Lenny hates; leaning carefully over Lenny he placed another log on the fire and farted. 'Sorry Lenny boy,' as the room filled with sprout perfume, Lenny raised his weary head his nose wiggled and buried its self in his tail.

'Well Mr Tibbs,' said the vet packing up his bag. 'Lenny has been one lucky dog, those are nasty bite marks, I've patched him up as best I can, he's a fighter, which probably saved his life; I'll see myself out.'

'We'll soon get you better Lenny boy,' Mr Tibbs stroking Lenny gently avoiding the bandaged areas.

Lenny licked Mr Tibbs hand, which took some effort as he rested his head back into his bedding.

'Don't you worry about me, Lenny boy,' Mr Tibbs looked down at Lenny with mixed emotions; Mr Tibbs was angry and a little tearful.

Mr Tibbs stood by the kitchen table and placed his hand on the rickety pine chair. Hanging on the back of it was the scruffy brown coat he'd found in the woods. Reaching in the pocket he took out the penknife and placed it on the table; Mr Tibbs held up the jacket to the window and examined the yellow marks on the sleeve.

'Same colour as the shower block paint, this is our man Lenny.'

Mr Tibbs picked up the penknife and looked closely at the picture of the caravan and the initials B.D. 'Stick an (A) in between those letters and that's our man, aye Lenny.' Lenny struggled to raise his head. 'Sorry boy, you keep still now.'

Mr Tibbs stared at the knife for a long time. 'I reckon Lenny boy that this here knife may belong to one of our traveller friends!

'It's very well made, and old, this here picture is one of them traditional caravans, very similar colour to the travelling caravans on my site.

Kinda knife handed down through generations I expect.'

Lenny was ignoring Mr Tibbs and hoping for some tea.

The travellers were welcomed every year; in return, they helped Mr Tibbs with the renovations, improvements and any maintenance on the site.

Mr Tibbs didn't know all the travellers personally as every year different families came; the travellers knew from their community that Mr Tibbs campsite was a welcome stay.

Every season the young families would come, with new generations of children and dogs. There had never been a problem, an argument or a disagreement - until now.

On the travellers' site, some of the men were tending to the horses three sturdy mares all of a similar colour yet in different ways, brown and white, all white and all brown.

The folks had a fire going and used old fashion pots to boil and cook, it was a special day, a traditional event where the community celebrated the old ways with special recipes, traditional clothing and playing music.

The camp was in good spirits, it was early afternoon and the smell from the fire pots was delicious and rich. Some of the older men had begun to create rhythm with their violins and mandarins, the children were dancing and the women sang as they prepared food.

The sun was out; the men chatted and smoked pipes as they groomed the horses.

One of the men spoke: 'I found him this morning muddy and feeling sorry for himself strolling up the narrow pass near the woods.' The men looked at the young black cross breed collie sitting under the old caravan the dog looked across at the men as if he knew he was the topic of conversation.

'Looks like a scrapper,' said another man.

'I - that's true, there was blood on his front as well as mud, he's fine though, it's not his blood. 'Better be careful with him he maybe a biter,' returned the other man.

The men were in high spirits, telling stories of adventure and romance; jugs of wine and tobacco pouches were passed around the camp fuelling extra loud bouts of laughter and a little drunkenness.

Mr Tibbs steered his old tractor their way and into the camp.

'Afternoon Mr Tibbs, care to share a brew!' said one of the men cheerfully.

Mr Tibbs did not look in the mood for joining the party, his look was stern, he approached the men with his chest puffed out, his head held high. He was carrying something large under his arm.

Mr Tibbs stood broadly clearing his throat and tapping his chest with his fist like an operatic singer about to audition; which caused him to belch loudly.

Composing himself Mr Tibbs forced the words out.. 'I have something here that may belong to someone in this here camp; I'm hoping someone can tell me who this here coat belongs to?' Mr Tibbs spread the coat out on the grass so everyone could see it.

The men pulled in and gathered round looking down at the coat; murmurs and soft talking followed; heads began to shake and some of the men returned to their original positions taking up their pipes and mugs.

Murmuring occurred such as:

'Not seen' – 'Never seen' – 'Ain't mine' – 'not is' – 'Never was' – 'Load of old rags' – 'needs washing.

One of the more senior looking men stood with hands on hips a stride of the coat and made a few muffled comments shaking his head.

'My, my' – 'Will ya look at dat' – 'Made of camel dat' – 'keep ya nice an' warm dat will.'

Mr Tibbs adjusted his stance, 'and leaned in on the man, 'do you know whose coat this is?'

'Can't say I do Mr Tibbs, nobody here claims ownership of dat there coat; it's well made though, it's a good coat Mr Tibbs.' The man carried on looking down at the coat as if waiting for it to get up and walk off.

Mr Tibbs produced the coats hidden contents; the gypsy men watched as the penknife Mr Tibbs had previously found landed softly in the centre of the coat.

The men again moved forward chattering to each other examining closely the object Mr Tibbs had thrown on the coat.

'Whose initials are B.D?' said Mr Tibbs studied each face in turn.

The men looked around at each other, mouths opening and shutting like gasping fish out of water they shook their heads and mumbled noises of confusion. 'Don't know '- 'Ta be sure' – Nowt ta do wid may.'

The small girl unseen by everyone knelt by the coat staring at the knife.

Ruby picked up the knife holding it palm open.

Mr Tibbs immediately took the knife from the girl, 'You mustn't play with Knives young lady; you might cut yourself.'

Mr Tibbs smiled gently at the little girl and held the knife a loft at arm's length, 'whose here knife is this!' he said stretching his lungs, bellowing like a giant.

The small soft voice so close yet faint answered Mr Tibbs question.

'It's mine sir,' said Ruby.

Mr Tibbs looked down at the little girl his arm still out stretched holding the knife high like the liberty statue torch.

Everyone else now turned their focus from the knife to the little girl.

Mr Tibbs lowered his arm, at first his face was full of frown and scowl he was about to be stern however Ruby's sweet face quickly changed his mind.

'What would a sweet little girl like you be doing with a knife?' Mr Tibbs bent low his hands rested on his knees.

'It belonged to my father sir, (Barney Dowel) he gave it to me before he died.' Ruby smiled at Mr Tibbs.

Mr Tibbs stared at Ruby, her eyes were wide as her smile; he knew without question she was telling the truth, his heart was melting, his eyes blinked.

Mr Tibbs handed over the Penknife gently. Mr Tibbs was confused, how did the knife come to be in the pocket?

Whilst bending low in thought something caught his eye, Mr Tibbs noticed the dark scruffy dog lying just beneath one of the caravans; immediately he shot a finger at the dog. Mr Tibbs could see it looked bloody and fresh from a scrap.

'Whose dog is this?' Mr Tibbs demanded renewed anger in his voice.

'We found him stray like,' said a man nearest the dog.

Mr Tibbs had a rush of blood to the head, he now felt very hot, and he also felt that he was being lied to and could no longer contain his frustration.

'I've had enough of this, someone is not telling me the truth, that dog attacked my dog and someone here is trying to ruin me.

'If no fella's is going to tell me the truth then I assumes you are all in it together; I don't know why; I've been more that fair to you folk over these years.' 'I want all of you off my site by end of week!' Mr Tibbs shouted.

'Please Mr Tibbs,' Begged Ruby.

Mr Tibbs pointed his finger firmly at everyone. The thought of poor Lenny had reminded him to be strong in his actions.

'I'm sorry young lady,' Looking down at Ruby; but that there's my final decision.'

Back at the upper fields not everyone was willing to forgive Mr Nutty Woodlander.

'I need to put things right and stop Mr Fingle from continuing to ruin this site; I've got some ideas, if you'll hear me out.' Nutty looked desperately at the gang for support and approval.

'Come on guys give me a chance.'

Chapter Eight
A Van Plan

There was frustration and sadness in the traveller's camp; for over fifty years - generations past had been coming to this camp way before it was a caravan park. Back then it was just farmland and Mr Tibbs was a small boy; his mother owned the farm and always welcomed the travelling community.

The men talked into the night, trying to make sense of what had happened.

'Clearly Mr Tibbs thinks we done the damage; but why would we sabotage our way of life here; we have nothing to gain, someone has set us up and wants us out,' said one of the men, the others agreed in murmured responses. 'Tis nowt but trouble' – ' Flamin', Flippin' terrible' – 'Be Jesus heaven help us.'

'Well it's worked, unless we can find out who and why; we're going have to leave, we don't want any trouble or Police involvement; we'll definitely get the blame,' said another man.

Ruby was close by listening; someone had taken her father's coat and knife and purposely put yellow paint on it but who? I can't let this happen, thought Ruby; she knew she had to do something before it was too late, she had some ideas and slipped away to find the gang.

Nutty was still in the doghouse. 'There must be something I can do to make things right?' pleaded Nutty.

'I think you've done enough for a long while,' Skye giving Nutty one of his fearless, tough, unforgiving looks.

'Arguing is not going to get us anywhere,' Becky gave Skye one of her parental scolding looks.

'Well if it wasn't for this traitor hiding those poaching scoundrels… we still don't know if he's really come clean; he could still be trying to fool us!' Skye raised his voice.

'That's enough,' said Hamish. 'We need to move on from this, we need to think.' 'Shouting and arguing won't help anyone.'

Nutty nudged slowly forward. 'Look guys I just need time to make things right.'

'Mr Fingle and his cronies still hide out in me most nights, poaching the woods; perhaps I could push myself over…and.'

Just then Ruby interrupted. 'I don't think that's a good idea and it won't help anyone especially you Nutty.'

Ruby continued: 'The best way to help is to listen for information, to find out if they have any more plans to vandalise the sight; have you heard anything lately?'

'No nothing lately, I know they're due to poach tonight, something about setting some traps,' said Nutty.

'Right, then we haven't got long to set our own trap,' said Ruby.

'Mr Tibbs thinks the damage to the site was done by my folks and has told us to leave by the end of the week.'

'That's darn wrong and below the belt,' said Cowboy shooting a stare at Nutty.

'I'll do my best to find out what I can,' said Nutty anxious to please.

'I have another idea to add, that may just move things along,' said Hamish.

'You and your friends can help Ruby.' 'Sure anything,' said Ruby eagerly.

'Good, this is what you'll need, gather round everyone.'

Much later that night the moonlight offered some assistance to the three men crouching low as they walked spidery through the long wet grass; their wellingtons made a synchronised swishing sound as they glided through the thickening, heading towards the woods.

'There it is,' whispered one of the men, his long wiry finger pointing at Nutty's position next to the woods. 'Is it me or does that caravan always seem to be in a different place?'

'It's you,' said the other man, 'either that or them trees are moving about.'

Two of the men wore identical flat caps, pressed low almost covering their shifty eyes, faces dark as soot with thick black wiry hair poking out like needles, they could be twins, the difference being, one was clean shaven and the other had a large moustache that looked like it was stuck on.

'Will you two pack it in,' Fingle turned on the two men spitting his words out, his teeth bared like a great white shark on the attack.

'Get in the caravan, draw down them blinds, light up and shut up,' Fingle ordered the men. Fingle wasn't a large man however he was built like a middleweight prize fighter- he had a nose like a Bulldog and a forehead with more creases than a tramp's blanket.

The three men entered the caravan; Nutty creaked and swayed as the men shuffled around in the darkness closing Nutty's blinds.

The lamp spread light from the ceiling across the walls slowly illuminating the small space, the three dark faces sat around the table huddled like coal miners down pit.

Unnoticed at first a shape in the middle of the table began to grow and spread as the last of the light filtered through and brightened up the room.

'What's this?' said one of the flat caps. 'It's some sort of model,' said Fingle his large forehead shadowing the cardboard and lifelike pieces, Fingle scanned every detail of the hand-crafted structure on the table.

'That's Tibbs's farm in the middle!' cried the other flat cap.

'Keep your voice down,' snarled Fingle bearing his yellow teeth, spit oozing through the large gap in his bottom row.

The model of Mr Tibbs farm was made from matches, cardboard, and sheep's wool. The grass made from felt garment; the cardboard walls were coloured in brick red, the trees made using real sticks with dyed cotton wool creating a miniature wood.

Fingle studied the model intensely; mumbling and dribbling as his eyes rolled and jostled back and forth his eyebrows roller coasting with his frown.

'Old Tibbsey has plans to expand and create some sort of happy holiday camp- football field – mountain bike route – café and picnic park; all very adventurous Mr Tibbs, but not if I have anything to do with it.' Fingle snarled and blew out a long huff of bad smelling air.

Flat caps pulled their necks in and held their breath for several minutes and then let go – 'Phew!' as they inhaled Fingle's egg and mustard dinner still partially stuck between his teeth.

'What's this?' flat cap (without moustache) held up a scrolled paper wrapped with bright yellow elastic banding.

Flat cap (with moustache) snatched the scroll, pulled off the band and spread out the paper; flat cap (without Moustache) bared teeth and frowned.

'It's a planning list for Tibbsey's model,' Moustache read out the list:

- *Mark out new road layout*
- *Dig foundations for café*
- *Order picnic furniture*
- *Hire digger for pond*
- *Order fencing and timber*

'What's this?' Moustache inched his face closer to the scroll, his eyes narrowed and his face twisted and changed from a painful grimace to a dirty murky smile.

'Give me that!' Fingle snatched the scroll from Moustache.

Moustache thought to argue for about half a second and the thought of that smelly breath baring and barking down on him changed his mind.

Fingle read out the large letters on the bottom of the page that were circled in red pen:

IMPORTANT
Dig out mother's consent deeds for planning authority.
In storage cupboard - In the old barn.

Fingle sat back. His eyebrows began a tennis match with the wrinkles on his forehead; the two flat caps closely observed the intense brow battle copying Fingle's facial movements.

Then came the self-inflicted boxing match as Fingle tapped at his forehead with his fist then at his teeth with his knuckles, finally a jubilant uppercut that narrowly missed Moustache.

'That's it!' cried out Fingle.

'Yes!'... Cried the Flat caps jubilantly hugging each other, but not really sure why.

'Shut up!' Fingle barked, spit flying, flat caps released themselves and wiped the spit from their faces.

'Right,' said Fingle running his eyes up and down the scroll, 'we're going to make a slight alteration to this here plan once we've found it; boys darken up your faces were going out tonight to the old barn.'

Back at Mr Tibbs cottage the old wooden mantel clock chimed just after 3 o'clock, Lenny was used to sleeping through the hourly chimes it was Mr Tibb's snoring that woke him.

Mr Tibbs shifted in the bed like a beached walrus wrestling with himself for a comfortable position. Lenny retreated to a safer spot behind the spare pillow and buried his nose in his tail.

Lenny's left ear automatically lifted into radar position this was normal for Lenny when Mr Tibbs disrupted his sleep.

Nightly noises from the outside yard would filter through Lenny's radar database:

(Owl – wind – creaky gate – Fox – Badger – Rat and so on).

Somewhere near the farm the gang was silent and waiting for a signal from Hamish.

'You cold Ruby?' Bobby asked offering his side door. 'I can put the gas on you could warm up while we wait?'

'Yeah thanks,' Said Ruby jumping in. 'We'll let you know when we get the signal,' said Bobby closing his door quietly.

Bobby caught Becky staring at him in approval; she smiled and kept her stare until Bobby straight-faced eventually smiled back.

'What time is it?' said Skye, struggling to keep still. 'It's just after 3 o'clock,' said Hamish.

Hamish had his best eye window fixed on the five-bar gate entrance to the farmyard; Cowboy shared Hamish's concentration, staring down the hill poised like a gun fighter facing his opponent, ice cool and steady as a world class snooker player.

Hamish had studied the landscape towards the gate and was now acutely aware of any small change in the darkness, he followed the pattern of the wind as the grass moved and tangoed with the moonlight.

'What was that?' whispered Skye doing his best Meer cat impression.

'Badger,' said Cowboy.

'Fox,' corrected Hamish.

Cowboy shot a stare at Hamish but didn't challenge his observation, returning his gaze back to the surveillance spot.

Hamish was like a statue only his satellite whirring softly.

Skye returned to his Meerkat position sweeping a glance behind him from left to right.

'Will you relax,' Said Cowboy.

'Easy for you to say, Mr cool Cowboy,' Skye mimicked a pair of pistols at his sides blowing out pretend bullets.

'Grow up,' said Bobby.

'How much longer?' Becky shuffled and rotated on the spot.

'I don't think anything's going to happen and I'm really tired.'

'No stamina,' said Cowboy spinning around. 'This is a stake out and we need to see it through, I'm trying to concentrate and you're…'

'Shadows right of the old oak,' said Hamish interrupting Cowboy.

Almost invisible three dark shapes flickered and twitched as they moved cautiously amongst the trees. Only the moon picked up their starts and stops and added a few dark inches to where they hid, the five-bar gate wobbled.

'Get ready, positions everyone,' said Hamish a most serious tone to his voice. 'Bad guys on the move.'

Chapter Nine
Movements in the Dark

Fingle and the two flat caps reached the back of old barn.

Larger than most barns more like an aircraft hangar, the doors were tall and solid oak bound together by a heavy chain. The only weakness was the padlock now rusty and brittle.

The men sat low pressing their backs to the doors their weight strained the padlock as it sat up in the chain like a shackled prisoner fragile and ready to break.

Fingle reached deep into his coat pocket and pulled out a short metal bar, clenching it tight he sat for a cautionary minute, staring at the cottage across the yard, waiting…

Fingle moved swiftly, the old lock was no match for the sturdy metal bar; the padlock fell free from its chains into Fingle's hand, quick as a ferret's bite they were in.

'They're in,' said Cowboy Sharpe eyed. 'Right let's move you know your positions,' said Hamish urgently.

The convoy rolled slowly down the hill from their hidden observation post, the gang had recently oiled and was almost silent – just the wind running past them blowing a wish.

The gang circled the yard and came in through the main tractor entrance, taking up position from the front as opposed to rear where the men had slipped in.

Hamish directed the gang in silence, nodding to Skye, Bobby and Becky.

The three of them took up positions gently pressing tight against the front exit of the old barn. The old doors moaned. 'Steady,' whispered Skye.

Fine lines of torchlight cut through the slats moving across from Becky to Bobby, the gang froze as the light paused over Skye and eventually died back within the barn, the men were busy within.

Hamish and Cowboy nodded at each other and made their way slowly to the rear exit.

The old barn held a vast amount of odds and sorts: an old car engine, a tin bath, a four poster bed, a flaky old telephone box, a petrol pump and even a grand piano more odds than sorts - Mr Tibbs wasn't one for throwing stuff away.

Fingle shot the torchlight in all directions searching for a cupboard or filing cabinet; he was looking for sorts – document sorts.

Flat cap with moustache made a hissing sound through his teeth and pointed with his nose at the large dresser in the corner.

The dresser was huge and looked like a small cathedral, ornamental glass and fine carvings framed the doors and drawers. 'This could be it,' whispered Fingle his beady eyes bursting forward.

Hamish and Cowboy were now at the rear and backed up steady against the doors, again the old barn groaned as the mighty doors held their breath.

Fingle jerked his head on a sideways slant 'what was that?' he whispered. Fingle froze in mid step his arms out stretched his eyes rolling like balls in a roulette wheel.

Flat caps were still moving toward the dresser only to find themselves in darkness as Fingle's torchlight deserted them.

'What's up?' hissed moustache catching his balance arms outstretched.

Fingle stood statuesque in the strangest position, signalling for attention his only movement was his right hand outstretched; his fingers were running along a pretend key board as if he were playing piano.

Flat caps looked at Fingle then back at each other and then at the old grand piano that lay just feet away.

Fingle stared at the flat caps as their gaze from the piano returned. 'Idiots didn't you here that noise?'

All three men now stood in awkward positions like forgotten show room dummies, silent and listening intently for any sound.

At the front of the old barn Ruby stepped out of Bobby and looked around the yard. 'Come straight back when the lights are on,' whispered Bobby.

Ruby nodded and made her way across the yard towards the flood light switch housed in a box on a post near the cottage.

Hamish and Cowboy had secured the rear doors, together the gang had locked down the old barn; Fingle and the flap caps were so far unaware of their entrapment.

Within the barn the three men had moved from their paralysed positions satisfied that any noise they heard must have been a rat or some other night rodents also on a night hunt.

Ruby tip toed a cross the yard towards the floodlight switch; jumping a small rockery, past the milk churns and around the woodpile. Ruby knew the layout of the yard well but it was darker than a witches' cat.

Overlooking the yard, the cottage was silent; the only sign of life was a tail of smoke chasing the wind as it left the chimney pot, the dying embers of the evening fire still keeping the sleepers within cosy and warm.

The yard was strangely silent considering all the activity it was hiding; the flood light switch box was a little taller that Ruby had expected she stretched and reached but even her buckle boots didn't have enough heel to allow the extra 3 or 4 inches she needed.

Ruby remembered passing the woodpile a small stump would give the step up she needed.

Ruby looked back and searched the darkness for the woodpile, trying to work out her last steps; she turned quickly going right then left, in her eagerness Ruby suddenly lost her balance.

Ruby's hands and elbows bravely offered themselves to inevitable pain as the blackness swallowed her up; the ground was cruel, cobbles and small stone pierced and dented her soft skin.

The pain arrived shortly; Ruby's thoughts instantly took her to her father's loving arms and his jolly smile he would pick her up with ease and kiss away the tears.

Ruby was a brave little girl, but right now she felt lost, needed help and wanted her dad.

Inside the cottage sleeping soundly Lenny was dreaming; his paws were barely touching the ground as he swept around the large oak tree he could smell the sweetness of the grasses and the tail of the grey and white rabbit he was gaining on and within a Hare's whisker.

In a flash and a blink, the rabbit had disappeared, Lenny had leapt to strike and was now tumbling into a flash of light and sound; Lenny's eyes opened fully following his nose that had followed his perked left ear.

Lenny's legs had not followed suit they were still spinning as he lay on his side like an overturned racing car.

Lenny wasn't sure what had woken him; his ears would tell him it was a very low-pitched sound like a silent scream. Lenny slipped off the bed and poked the curtains with his nose, everything in order? - His nose told him that something was not right, his ears agreed.

'There's nothing here,' cried Fingle throwing the last pile of old newspapers back in the drawer. 'Time we were out of here I gotta bad feeling about this place.' Fingle scowled, blew out his cheeks and kicked an old wicker basket.

Moustache agreed. 'Yeah I'm starting to feel (Claustro - what sits) in this place.'

Fingle and the flat caps moved quickly towards the rear doors, checking about them as they hastened towards their exit.

Reaching the end Fingle pushed on the old wooden doors expecting an immediate exit and was surprised to be knocked back; Fingle bad tempered as always attacked pushing again with all his might, but was again met by the unyielding wood.

Beckoned by Fingle the flat caps joined in and all three men shouldered with their entire force and drive, pushing and stabbing at the old doors. Wood and man fought for several minutes, wood creaked and groaned, gasped and moaned - doors stood fast, superior and unmoved.

'We've been locked in,' Fingle snapped. 'Quick let's try the other end there must be another way out?' Fingle drew in a breath and began running, the torch light danced around the barn as Fingle swung his arms about trying to steady the stream of diminishing torch light ahead of him.

Flat caps followed, tripping and stumbling as they struggled to keep up with Fingle and his fading light.

'Good job Cowboy,' said Hamish. 'Yeah let's hope them boys don't find a large rabbit hole the other end,' said Cowboy grinning.

'Little Ruby will be hitting the flood lights just about now,' said Hamish looking a tad nervous. Cowboy moved from the doors and peered around the side; it was still pitch dark in the yard.

Bobby, Becky and Skye could hear the commotion within and were waiting for impact their end. 'Get ready,' said Skye.

The impact wasn't very effective; Fingle had very little energy left after his 300 metre obstacle dash. Flat caps were lost and still stumbling in circles after losing their guiding light; Moustache found the entrance to the old red telephone box running straight into it, the old phone bell rang out as he hit his head on the receiver – knock out!

The old barn fell silent for what seemed like several minutes. Bobby and Becky looked at each other; they were both expecting another assault on the door.

Nothing - except for a dull thumping sound.

'You hear that?' said Skye. Becky and Bobby nodded. 'You two stay here I'm going to check it out,' Skye crept around to the side cautiously.

Skye was just in time to see a dark figure cut through the side of the old barn, the figure threw something to one side; someone was escaping and had found a weak spot in the barn's belly.

'Darn it!' said Skye, 'one of them is getting away.'

Fingle had managed to find a loose panel and wasn't going to wait for his cronies to follow; it was every man for himself. Stumbling outside he made his way cunningly across the yard his rat like senses were guiding him through the twists and turns; only his yellow teeth could be seen; his torch light had finally died.

Ruby wiped her face with her forearm; her hands were stinging, just like the time when she fell into a bed of nettles last summer. She gently pressed her hands together and rubbed slowly to remove the stones from her soft skin.

Ruby didn't see the staggered movements of the shape as it closed in; the shape that easily covered her small frame; only her bright blue eyes stood out sparkling like lone star's in the night, but she was not alone.

Chapter Ten
Friend or Foe

Lenny was dreaming again his short legs were scratching on the duvet as he ran for his life through the open field. This time Lenny was running not after the rabbit, but from the rabbit; Lenny's rabbit had grown to a very large size, at least tenfold from his previous encounter and was now fast approaching him.

Lenny quick thinking took refuge underneath one of the caravans; the giant rabbit lunged forward his paws snatched at Lenny's tail as Lenny scrambled under the caravan and out of reach of the giant fur ball. The rabbit managed to squeeze its ugly head under the van inches away from Lenny who was now cowering in-between an old deck chair and a deflated beach ball.

The giant nose had a life of its own padding around like a feeling hand, Lenny held his breath, suddenly the giant nose paused and perked up, the rabbit new exactly where Lenny was. Lenny thought he was safe surely the rabbit was too big to move any further.

Suddenly the caravan began rocking, and lifting, Mr Rabbit was growing in size.

Lenny had nowhere to go, the giant fluff ball was inching forward as the caravan lifted; Lenny could see his own terrified reflection in the gigantic pink eyes the gleaming white fangs were huge, Lenny was rabbit food.

Lenny held his breath one last time and was surprised to hear a loud voice,

'Do you mind!' bellowed the voice from above. 'Get away with you!' the voice demanded even louder.

The rabbit was most startled; confused, it quickly backed out from underneath the caravan and almost immediately began shrinking. Lenny watched as the rabbit shrank until it was half Lenny's size it then sat up on its hind legs took a quick look around and ran off over a hill and completely out of sight.

Lenny came out from beneath the caravan, cautiously he looked about him and above him; there was no one in sight- Just Lenny and the caravan.

Lenny woke from his dream it was still dark, the duvet had covered Lenny completely where Mr Tibbs had left the bed.

Lenny dropped down from the bed still a little shaken and exhausted from his giant rabbit dream. Where had his master gone? Lenny peered through the curtains just as the floodlight lit up the yard, causing Lenny to step back and adjust his vision.

Mr Tibbs had activated the floodlights and was stood over Ruby. 'What on earth are you doing out here child?' said Mr Tibbs as he tightened up his red gown cord around his blue gown, wearing a slipper on one foot and a boot on the other.

Ruby explained all she could to Mr Tibbs about how Fingle and the flat caps had been the ones who vandalised the shower block. 'They were looking to ruin Mr Tibbs and take over his land.

Ruby went on to explain about the trap her and her friends had set to catch them by building a model of the Farm and making up a pretend document for the planning office.

This would make them think that Mr Tibbs had his mother's approval document for the planning office hidden in the old barn.

The plan was then to trap Finagle and the flat caps in the barn and wake Mr Tibbs by turning on the floodlights.

Ruby told the story quickly. Mr Tibbs looked quite exhausted after taking in Ruby's full story.

'Right then young lady you wait right here for me and I will see what we have in my barn.'

Mr Tibbs marched across the yard stopping briefly to pick up a long-handled shovel from the coalhouse.

Hamish and Cowboy waited for Mr Tibbs to get closer before moving away from the doors and parking up close by and out of sight.

The flood light switch also activated the barn lights, flat caps were still trying to make their way towards the back door falling over each other in the panic to get out. Moustache reached the back door first; Mr Tibbs introduced him to the flat end of his shovel right between the eyes.

Moustache fell backwards onto his pal; flat caps lay on the barn floor like a couple of upturned wood louse, struggling pathetically.

'Where's your mate – Fingle?' Mr Tibbs demanded, pointing his shovel like soldier with his rifle.

'We don't know Mr Tibbs,' flat caps spluttered, 'we lost him several minutes ago; it was all his idea Mr Tibbs, we was bullied into this,' flat caps pleaded and wined pathetically.

'Tell it to the police, barked Mr Tibbs. 'They're on the way, you two don't move or I'll be using this shovel to bury the pair of you.'

Flat caps had well and truly surrendered and were busy arguing about what their mothers would say.

The gang had all moved away from the barn and met together on the upper fields.

'Good work guys,' said Hamish a little puffed out. 'Ruby's OK she's explained everything to Mr Tibbs.'

'What happened to Fingle? He was at your end of the barn,' said Hamish concerned.

'We're not sure,' said Becky. 'Bobby thinks he may have escaped through a gap in the barn and slipped away before the floodlights came on.'

'We can't let him get away! Snapped Hamish. 'Right spread out gang we need to find him and box him in, Skye and Cowboy you take the lower field, Bobby, Becky the woods, I'll check the hedge rows.' Hamish had a determined look in his front windows.

Lenny sniffed the air high catching an unfamiliar sent a little like Mr Tibbs cooked breakfast yet strangely stronger, there was no bacon or eggs more curtains and carpet.

Cowboy with his keen senses noticed it first. The cottage had a flickering of bright colours red and yellow within the downstairs windows.

'Hold your horses!' yelled Cowboy. 'Look yonder the cottage is on fire!'

'Where's Ruby?' said Becky.

'I think she's with Mr Tibbs,' Bobby replied nervously.

Skye took the high ground and scanned the yard.

'She's not with Mr Tibbs,' shouted Skye.

Just then in the distance an engine was heard revving all ears and eyes shot in that direction.

Cowboy was first to the dirt track leading northward beside the woods, the tyre tracks were clear and broad – deep tread and heavy.

Hamish joined Cowboy and the others followed.

In the distance, the old Land rover rocketed a long bouncing and jostling on the dirt road with no lights on; Fingle was fighting with the steering wheel as the old truck moved side to side refusing to drive straight.

Ruby lay in the back tied tightly with an old red dressing gown cord.

Hamish turned around quickly as the cries at the cottage echoed across the yard.

'This is not what I planned,' Hamish looked shocked and not sure where to turn, the night was also turning…. ugly.

'What have I done?' Hamish looked across at the cottage as the silent night was shattered by the arrival of the travelling folk yelling and hollering.

Hamish tore off along the track desperate and confused coming to a halt in a ditch he looked back at the others anguished and beaten he threw himself into the woods and disappeared.

'Hamish!' 'Where are you going?' shouted Becky her broken voice turned to tears.

Lenny was tired, the bedroom floor appeared to move, it looked foggy and felt particularly warm, what's going on thought Lenny as he lay low stretching out near the window; Lenny closed his eyes.

Chapter Eleven
Nowhere to Hide

Fingle steered the Land rover sharply down a narrow lane stabbing a stare at the rear-view mirror he forced the long gear stick down a notch and slowed abruptly taking his foot off the gas pedal, breaking hard he turned down a steep drive and drove directly into a long garage, he sat for a few minutes the engine chattered and hummed and finally died as he pulled the key out of the dash board.

Hamish sat low in the bracken his tyres deflated as his satellite went on over drive.

'How could I be so stupid?' Hamish said out loud.

'Think! – Think!' – Think! ... Pop!'

'You called!' said Pop appearing from nowhere.

'Pop, Pop!' said Hamish hysterically.

'Son if you keep repeating my name I'm going to reupholster your insides and detach your satellite dish to your rear bumper!'

'I've messed up big time sir, Ruby's been kidnapped and it's my entire fault,' said Hamish propping himself against a log.

'We need to have a chat son,' Pop sighed.

Back on the hill. 'He could be anywhere in those woods,' protested Bobby.

'We need to do something about the fire!' yelled Skye.

'We need to find Hamish!' cried Becky.

'No!' Bobby looked at Becky sternly. 'Skye is right we need to
help put out that fire, Hamish is not here to lead us;
he's let us down when we needed him most!'

'Right we need to think quick and fast!' said Cowboy turning sharply towards the burning cottage.

'What are we going to do?' said Becky desperately.

'I've got a triple loading 8 pint holding, air pumped mega force 10, fire hosed injection, torpedo loaded – water gun... and I intend to use it!' Cowboy locked and loaded, rolled on towards the cottage.

Mr Tibbs had left the flat caps huddled in the barn rapped in chicken wire like packed sandwiches in cellophane their night was over.

Mr Tibbs re-entered the yard when suddenly several of the travelling men ran past him; his yard filled by the men from all directions; like a pitch invasion at Devon united the men were everywhere.

'Mr Tibbs sir, we need a water supply and quick sir!' said one of the men in urgency standing toe to toe with Mr Tibbs.

'Right away sir, there's no time to waist.'

'Lenny!' cried Mr Tibbs looking up stunned at the site of his cottage in flames.

Lenny raised an eye lid his nose twitched uncontrollably all his senses were on red alert but he didn't know why.

The bedroom door appeared to glow from all ends and a thick blanket of black smoke crept under much like the giant rabbit paw Lenny had seen in his dream. Is this a dream? Lenny thought, his senses were telling him otherwise.

Holly bush was a hive of activity – it was deep into the night and the early hours slowed with the drama unfolding.

It could be bonfire night on the farm lots of figures shouting and jostling around – flickering torch light dancing around the yard like sparklers and in the centre flames were reaching out of Mr Tibbs cottage window flapping at the night air.

'How are you going to put that fire out with an 8-pint water pistol!' shouted Skye.

'You'll see, come on all of you we need to work together and fast!' Cowboy drew his gun and headed to the rear of the cottage and higher ground.

Cowboy had a hose pipe fitted to his gun which was directly linked to his water tank – plugged in and charged up he let loose the mega force 10 jet of powerful water – by this time the down stairs windows had cracked and flames were bursting out – the impact of the water caused a surge of smoke and hissing as the flames cowered.

'It's working!' cried Becky.

'Keep it going Cowboy pistol whip those flames!' shouted Skye.

Suddenly as fast as the stream of water hit the surging flames the jet of water died to a trickle.

The flames saw their chance to regroup and relight with full strength – bellowing out in defiance of Cowboys shoot out.

'Quick!' yelled Cowboy. 'Skye plug this into your tank.'

Cowboy pumped the mega force 10 – reloaded and fired another jet of water at the enemy flames. 'Yee Ha!'

'Hamish lad you're a fine young man and a caring sort that's for sure – all good leaders find it hard at times when best laid plans go up in smoke.' Pop pulled in close to Hamish.

'Let's look at this logically and clear our minds,' Pop closed his shutters his satellite dish humming and making strange noises.

Hamish hesitantly copied Pop and closed his shutters.

After a few minutes Pop awoke from his meditation and humming noises.

'Right lad!' said Pop loudly. Hamish opened his shutters startled and wide-awake finding Pop's nose pressed to his nose.

'Answer me this Hamish lad?'

'*When a snake ventures from its home to seek and find its prey how far will it travel before night turns to day?*'

Hamish threw himself into thinking hard his front end scrunched and his satellite whirred once again.

'The snake returns...home... before dark... Fingle has Ruby at his farm...somewhere... he's gone back to his place!' yelled Hamish.

'Of course he has Hamish lad – you've figured it out, now what are you going to do?'

'I have a plan and I'll need the gang, thank you Pop.'

'You have it in hand Hamish lad – no need to thank me, now get on with you and find that girl!'

Lenny lay flat on the rug near the window he was acutely aware of all the shouting and hollering from outside. Lenny was finding it hard to breath his sense of smell was off the scale as the unwanted fumes poured into his black button nostrils.

Lenny began feel sleepy again struggling to push his body any lower to the ground he inched his way forward to the window pane and struggled to scratch the glass; it looked busy outside and different lights changed between different figures in the yard – for a second Lenny thought he saw Mr Tibbs Lenny new that something bad was going to happen and suddenly felt happy and not alone it was time to sleep now, time to chase that rabbit over the hill for a long way.

'That's the last tank empty, not a drop left and no water supply that will reach the gun hose,' Bobby looked at Becky desperately.

The cottage was still re igniting after every water tank change – the gang had nearly put the fire out but nearly wasn't good enough and the fire would not give up its relentless quest to burn the cottage down.

Suddenly a familiar voice joined the gang.

'My tanks full – plug me in!' said Hamish fire in his voice as he frowned at the flames.

From the inside in Mr Tibbs bedroom Lenny lay motionless his paws lay gently on the window ledge which was flat to the floor, like an ornament placed specifically Lenny lay still his chest rose once more and then ceased to raise again.

From outside the window a large pole shaped frame descended swiftly forward impacting hard against the glass; small pieces shattered and showered Lenny like a spray of diamonds covering his fur, Lenny was dressed with particles of glass and wood; Lenny lay very still.

Large grubby hands immediately surged forward through the broken window; Lenny's body raised high onto Mr Tibbs shoulder as they descended the ladder.

'Give him to me!' shouted one of the men meeting Mr Tibbs at the bottom of the ladder.

Holding Lenny gently in his arms the man ran to nearest water holding and dipped Lenny down deep into the water leaving him under for several seconds.

Mr Tibbs looked startled and pushed forward to save his pal, the other men stopped him abruptly.

'No Mr Tibbs,' said a man. 'Let him do this, he knows what he's doing, trust him, please sir.'

Mr Tibbs waited breathless a look of anguish and fear, his face aged, his eyes welled and blinked; seconds seemed like hours.

Lenny rose from the water holding he felt so light as if he could fly - well I'll catch that rabbit now, thought Lenny.

Lenny's eyes opened and he could see thousands of twinkling stars the moon beamed at him and shot a smile, Lenny wagged his tail and coughed a bark.

'Thank God,' said Mr Tibbs.

The fire was finally out as the gang gathered their energy.

'Glad to see you boss,' said Skye.

No rest gang we have to find Ruby, let's move!' Hamish was focused.

The gang had been travelling for an hour when they approached the iron gate, barely hanging to its posts it was high and roped with barbed wire with a slide bar and pad lock keeping it together.

'How are we going to get through this gate? It looks solid,' said Becky looking around cautiously.

'Stand clear,' ordered Skye as he gracefully spun round like an elegant dancer his tow bar cracked precisely at the centre of the gate slide bar – a crack appeared and the bar fell softly to the leafy ground.

'Wow that was great!' Becky looked up as the gates eased open.

'I'm taking my red belt in caravan Kendo next week, which involves silent ninja manoeuvres in the dark,' said Skye proudly.

Chapter Twelve
Unlucky for Some

'What's that smell? Cowboy looked inquisitive.
'Silent manoeuvres in the dark, said Bobby smirking.
'Bobby! Becky scorned at her brother.
'Gang! Shush, Land rover a head,' ordered Hamish.

The gang approached the rotten old farm; junk lay everywhere fences in disrepair – an old tractor lay half rusted in a ditch – the house had no light and the land around was grassless and spoiled with mud and ditches.

Hamish remembered what Pop has taught him and closed his shutters.

'What's he doing?' whispered Bobby.

Hamish took a deep breath and opened his shutters focused his windows and pointed to the long building at the side of the house.

'Ruby's in there and time is short- Fingle will be in the house packing for a long drive, the back door of the Land rover is open and there are bags in the back.'

Ruby was sat in the dark tied to an old rickety chair which was in turn tied to a support post at the back of the garage.

Several times Ruby had tried to struggle free, a creaking could be heard whenever she attempted to pull forward; the garage was weak, tired and dangerous.

Shards of light were beginning to break through as day light exposed the wrecked garage and all its weak points.

The gang huddled around the garage and peered through several gaps where boards had fallen some were hanging on by a single rusty nail.

'I can see Ruby!' said Bobby in a low husky voice trying to be quiet.

In Bobby's excitement he leaned to hard, the boards gave way easily and Bobby quickly found himself inside the garage covered in rotten wood.

Ruby startled but relieved to see Bobby wriggled furiously in her chair, her head poked upwards as if she were trying to tell Bobby something.

'Don't worry Ruby, I'll get you out of here,' Bobby moved forward awkwardly and found himself stuck to gain further ground.

Ruby became more frantic in her movements her chin nodding up and down furiously.

Bobby pulled himself forward when an awful creak sounded out, a delayed echo filled the stale air – something bad was happening.

Bobby had been caught unawares by the main joist in the roof a long piece of wood that supported most of the rotting corrugated roof.

The roof wasn't particularly heavy but what lay undisturbed and frequently put upon on top were large amounts of stolen led pipe.

Bobby realised in time what was happening and fired himself forward his side door opening as he turned on his side and swallowed Ruby up into the safety of his front room with cushioned seating area.

Heavy pipe, timber and generally rotten filth fell onto Bobby denting his sides and cracking a window.

'Bobby!' yelled Becky.

The dust settled, the gang tore through the rubble, clearing away the heavy materials on poor Bobby's side.

'Can you stand?' Hamish beckoned the others to hitch under Bobby and tilt him back on his wheels.

'I'm OK!' Bobby's crockery, plates and dishes fell back into place within. 'You OK in there?' said Bobby concern in his voice.

Silence for a few seconds – 'I'm fine Bobby – thanks to you,' said Ruby.

Becky beamed with pride at her brother, who caught her look and smiled tight lipped.

Just then an engine roared. More dust erupted as the Land rover shot past the gang and skidded through the gates however colliding badly against a post the Land rover appeared to lose control before smoke bellowed from the front end.

The gang high tailed up the lane; on reaching the Land rover its occupant was gone the driver's door buckled and twisted, Fingle had chewed his way out and made off through the woods.

The gang followed. Cowboy tracked his trail back to Holly bush were all eyes were scanning for Ruby and Fingle.

Somewhere nearby Nutty had been watching and waiting patiently while his new friends had been busy Nutty had been hoping a certain snake may return to another familiar hiding place; he wasn't disappointed.

Hiding beneath Nutty Fingle wrestled with the damp grass on his back, his eyes scanning the woodland floor for any movement his way.

He kicked away the half empty pots of yellow paint that were stacked at the front end of Nutty's under carriage, stretching the cramp out of his legs.

Fingle grimaced in pain as he wriggled and twitched trying to find a painless position underneath Nutty; he let out a groan as he caught his toe on one of Nutty's adjustable feet.

Suddenly he heard a creek; Fingle froze, his eyes pieced forward as if on stems, the creaking sound came with a distinct drop of Nutty's undercarriage, Fingle's nose was now touching the cold metal of the caravan.

Fingle couldn't move, Nutty lowered his belly another inch, Fingle had to take a deep breath his back now pressing firmly to the ground lucky for him the muddy grass allowed just enough room to breathe;

Fingle was trapped, sandwiched between Caravan and grass.

Becky was first to hear Fingle's muffled cries and approached Nutty who was quiet and almost unseen in the woodland.

'Nutty you've caught Fingle?'

'Yes, he thought he could hide out underneath me until sun up and slip away!' Nutty sounded very upset and angry; his front windows were welling up.

'It's OK Nutty you've done a great job,' Becky said looking a little worried.

'It's not OK though is it?' Nutty creaked slightly.

Fingle let out a high-pitched wail as he spluttered for breath.

The rest of the gang had arrived. Becky spoke very softly and calm.

'Nutty has Fingle trapped underneath him, there's not much room for him to breath, and Nutty's very upset and would like our support to know what to do next.' Becky looked at Hamish with concern.

Hamish edged forward slowly.

'Nutty, you need to jack up a little pal.'

'I want to make things right,' Nutty spluttered. 'I just wanted to have friends, I watched you guys from a far and I ... I just wanted to join in and be one of the gang, I need to make it right and this low life used me.'

'Steady now Nutty,' said Hamish.

'Listen pal, you've got nothing to prove.

Life's choices sometimes happen in waves sometimes a bad one crashes through and for a while we get carried away; but we learn from this and we move on.'

Hamish looked at the others for support everyone nodded in agreement.

Hamish continued.

'Nutty, right now you have a choice to make, to do the right thing and take responsible action; when you let go of bad feelings they let go of you.'

Hamish had that serious look on.

'Were all here for you Nutty and that's our choice, right guys?' the gang nodded again.

Lenny heard Fingle's high pitched wail as it caught the night wind; he ran past Mr Tibbs yelping as if to say; 'follow me, that's our man.'

Mr Tibbs knew Lenny was onto Fingle and flagged down a police car at the scene.

Lenny ran towards the woods barking furiously. Lenny could see several lights and many figures as he arrived at the scene.

The men gently lowered Nutty to the ground torchlight shone in all directions, now joined by the blue lights of the police car.

Lenny was very excited and barked even louder at Fingle who lay slumped against a tree clutching his ribs and demanding a doctor.

Flat caps were cuffed and in the back seat of the police car now shuffled over to make room for their flattened pal.

'There you are Ruby!' said one of the men, picking Ruby up in his arms.

'Mr Tibbs sir,' said the tall man, 'while we were looking for Ruby our dog was attacked by a large rogue badger, we think it may have been the same animal that hurt your Lenny.

Mr Tibbs moved closer. 'Ruby,' he said softly, his stubble round face smiled broadly. 'Your father would be very proud of you,' Mr Tibbs looked a little glazed in the eyes as he patted her on the head.

The light show faded as everyone left. The police car drove steadily through the gates onto the road; its contents were silent, faces grey and sweaty like worn out socks.

Mr Tibbs and Lenny strolled back to what was left of the cottage.

'Looks like we have some work to do tomorrow, Lenny boy!'

Looks like we're sleeping in the barn, thought Lenny.

The gang were back on the high field watching the travelling men return to their camp with Ruby.

Nutty came over and sat with them quietly.

Becky nudged him and pulled a face, the gang had a new member; the summer seemed a long way off, Holly bush remained quiet for a while until tomorrow or the next day.

Author's Note

A long, long time ago when traveller families first crossed into faraway lands - it was the faithful caravan that took them on adventures over continent and sea, roads were fraught with danger impassable and treacherous — avalanches and landslides were common on every twist and turn; most roads were all but dirt, gravel and hard stone.

The traveller depended on his carriage it had to be strong and well-made wheels as tough as steel plating, axel as solid as flint rock and under carriage unbreakable. The weary traveller needed complete faith in his caravan to survive the desolate road. If the baron path beat or broke any part of the van then the driver would surely die stranded in no man's land.

Caravans and Romany travellers go back hundreds of years. The very first caravans were made from wood and metal found in the homeland of Eire, where tree roots bore deep into mines of unfound Copper ore and magical blue clay.

These caravans were built and fixed with a special compound taken from the blue clay and the root of the Larch tree - travellers called it - the magical stuff and named it Ropemel.

A secret of Mother Nature, Ropemel was the strongest and most flexible compound known to man – it would glow and sparkle when found deep within the mines and rock face – it was the best kept secret of the Romany people and all were sworn to an oath of silence.

Ropemel was used to build all traditional traveller caravans – like special glue Ropemel soaked into every part of the caravan.

This made the caravans strong, unbreakable and reliable for long-distance travel.

Legend foretold of caravans made with Ropemel bringing good luck.

Stories told of terrible storms and the darkest of nights where the way ahead was all but lost; on such nights it was said a voice could be heard from within the wind guiding the weary travellers to a safe place.

Legend told that it was the magic of Ropemel a life force now deep within the caravan itself.

Traveller families told these stories from all across Europe and Eire.

Today almost forgotten and only mentioned in celebration of fable and tradition.

However somewhere near the south coast give or take a mile or two; young Romany children have new stories to tell about modern caravans and a different kind of magic – one such story is to be found in the most beautiful quiet part of rural England although not that quiet.

Holly Bush Holiday Park is a small caravan park near the south coast of Devon close to the pretty seaside town of Teignmouth a little hidden and off the beaten track.

To find this postage stamp corner of England leave the fast roads for the slow village of Kendall – past the pub 'The pie and Pint,'

and 'Daisy Mays - Fill and Spill'- the grocery shop; that'll be the last shops and village for at least 10 miles.

Follow the south road and take the shade through the trees around the pond – 'Ducks dip'.

Carry on half a pig's ear, slow and steady sharp right turn into Rabbits foot lane. Carry on for a squirrel's chinwag just short of Hatchets Chicken farm.

Holly bush is still a goose feathers mile to the east. You can't miss it unless you've pushed on past the snail museum (easily missed) and crossed over Rickety bridge (you don't want to do that) Careful reversing you may get stuck in ploughman's dike and need a tow out.

The Nearest tractor pull will be Barking mud farm – a ferret's toe up the road.

The owner of Holly Bush holiday Caravan Park is Mr Tibbs, the farmer. He is aged three owls and a badger, which is about 45 years old in Devonshire-speak. He has no chin, and is well rounded with small feet, which are lost beneath his tummy. So he looks like a giant, free-range egg on legs.

Mr Tibbs usually starts the day in a pair of clean, blue overalls; but by the evening these are usually covered in thick oil, as he spends most of his time trying to fix his old tractor and getting stuck in the engine housing accidently knocking the support arm off the bonnet and subsequently ending up as a tractor sandwich. Mr Tibbs has a faithful dog 'Lenny' who painfully watches his master and cringes and whines when Mr Tibbs gets eaten by his tractor -

Lenny is a small scruffy, hairy Jack Russell with dark yellow fur. He is fast, fearless, and yaps a lot. Lenny barks at the postman, the butcher, the milkman, the paperboy and the AA break down man; the AA man is often at the Caravan Park to help fix the tractor. He has a yellow van. Yellow is Lenny's least favourite colour, ever since Mr Tibbs accidentally spilt 15 beaten eggs all over him, his fur was bright yellow for a week and the smell – phew!

Like most caravan parks Holly bush closes from October to April: Known as the off season, - yes rain and mud.

During this period at Holly bush - there are only a small number of people still on site this includes a small community of travellers who in return for their stay help Mr Tibbs to fix and improve the site.

On the lower field is the old farm cottage where Mr Tibbs and Lenny live together. Lenny sleeps in the old piggery but sneaks in during the winter - cosy by the open fire, his little tail tucked in - as it took ages to grow the fur back when he accidently burnt it last winter.

The farm cottage has a large yard with lots of small sheds and housing mainly filled with rubbish and old furniture.

Holly bush camp site is spread across three fields and surrounded by woodland, river and hedging. The caravans are spread out in order of shape, size and age. Some are small, some are big, some are super - new, and some are falling apart and need towing away and scrapping!

The caravans at Holly bush are different from your average van which is where the Romany magic comes back into the story.

In the open fields, the caravans sit in ranks. In the upper fields are the biggest caravans: 'The Hobbies.' All the Hobbies are similar in size and length however one stands out amongst the rest.

A customised head-van extended 8-berth capacity 'Royal conqueror 840 special' otherwise known as 'Tank'.

Tank is not in 'the gang' he has his own crew and does his own hanging around: Looking down on everyone else, telling everyone else how great he is.

In the lower fields sit the older caravans some more than fifty years old still in use - With grand old names like: Ambassador GT 1920

– Dorchester 590 and Premiere 640.

Tired, discoloured and worn, however wise and watchful grandparents – the oldest (Buccaneer Stirling) known as 'Pop'- with hubcaps still shiny and proud like old war medals he tells stories of the old war, surviving the bombs and fighting off the scrap metal dealers Pop advices the younger caravans on waxing, oiling, waterproofing and the correct tyre pressure.

Finally, the middle field – this is where the 'Gang' live: (Night Star 350) known as 'Skye' – a two-year-old blue - 3 birth with retractable awning – loud, proud and built in the Newcastle Skye has all the channels including The Disney club, scrap metal challenge and DIY SOS caravan repairs – the big build.

Skye is keen to impress and likes to look sharp and in good shape – he does martial arts and has a blue belt in caravan kendo – which he attends on Sunday mornings in the lower fields where Japanese import 'Kicky yo towbar' teaches all the young vans.

The twins: Both (Delta twin 22's) known as 'Bobby and Becky,' Becky five minutes older than Bobby off the production line

(Doesn't let him forget it) Inseparable however very different Bobby thoughtless and rude Becky polite and honest.

The twins are always fighting and disagree on most things – Bobby thinks that he is right all the time and likes to tell his sister exactly that most days. Bobby is an expert on everything to do with hip hop, garage, rap and new wave sole – he's down with the kids and likes to think he's the new MD, MM, MMM and MNM.

Becky: Sensible, reliable dependable, commendable, appreciative, believable, achievable, argumentative, imaginative, likable, debateable. She doesn't do: cruelty, deliberate, harmful, blameful, rudeness, impoliteness, silliness, unkindness, judgemental, bias, blameless, ambiguous, opinionated or obnoxious – just plain sensible. Becky likes to read- study and learn about how things work in general; relentlessly inquisitive she also likes to see the good in most people and caravans – helping others is rewarding and honourable.

(Californian 45): Known as 'Cowboy' a young import from the wild west of America. Cowboy is cool, level headed and quick on the move a good all-round team player. Originally from Dallas Texas – Cowboy likes to hustle and rustle, practicing his herding skills with the 2 sheep and 1 goat on site - using anyone's washing line to practice lassoing and whooping – which apparently go together.

Cowboy hasn't got a gun licence which he insists he needs for his 'triple loading 8 pint holding, air pumped – mega force 10 – fire hosed injection – torpedo loaded – water gun.'

Finally, the leader of the caravan gang: Hamish. A Scottish (Ranger 660) made in Glasgow Scotland, Hamish has tartan curtains and is full of Scottish pride. He is very brave and responsible young trailer van with a heart the size of one of his large cushions on the back seats – well it's big and soft and full of squidgy stuff and everyone feels very comfortable around him.

Hamish loves the caravan site – especially the off season and days when things are not so quiet, peaceful or ordinary. Hamish is always ready to lead his gang to the next adventure or into deep trouble.